Mary Poppins

This volume examines *Mary Poppins* as a 1960s film reflecting and invested in its radically changing times, a largely but not unmitigatedly antiestablishment musical resonant with conditions and issues powerfully affecting baby boomers.

Among the explosion of baby boomer films that rocked the 1960s, the most stirring early work was likely *Mary Poppins*. This 1964 film captivated young audiences, earning top-grossing ticket sales, multiple Oscars, and landmark status as a cultural phenomenon. The book illuminates *Mary Poppins* as a musical teeming with preoccupations of American youth in the early-to-mid-1960s, including antiestablishment desires, anxieties, and pleasures. Reading against the dominant grain, this book deciphers *Mary Poppins* as a mid-century reflection that spans the generation gap, the dysfunctional nuclear family, youth unrest, activism including feminist advocacy, counterculturalism, capitalist imperialism, race relations, socially conscious music, and hallucinogenic consciousness expansion. Conjunctively, the book explores tensions inherent in this studio production as a mainstream Disney release evoking imperatives of 1960s American youth while sanitizing figures and values representing radical change. Further, examining the film's collective authorship, this volume traces *Mary Poppins'* origins in the writings and life of nonconformist author P.L. Travers as well as in Disney cinema and the studio's adaptation processes. Analysis extends to diverse facets of *Mary Poppins'* reception, including the shifting image of its star, Julie Andrews, the film's influence on popular culture and controversy among some as an adaptation, its appropriation by drug culture, association with the teenpic, and status as cinema of social consciousness.

This book is ideal for students, researchers, and scholars of cinema studies and youth culture.

Leslie H. Abramson is a Visiting Scholar at the American Bar Foundation. Abramson, a film scholar, is the author of *Hitchcock and the Anxiety of Authorship* as well as book chapters and journal essays on cinema in the 1960s, law and film, and Hitchcock. She holds a Ph.D. from the University of Chicago, Illinois.

Cinema and Youth Cultures

Cinema and Youth Cultures engages with well-known youth films from American cinema as well as the cinemas of other countries. Using a variety of methodological and critical approaches the series volumes provide informed accounts of how young people have been represented in film, while also exploring the ways in which young people engage with films made for and about them. In doing this, the Cinema and Youth Cultures series contributes to important and long-standing debates about youth cultures, how these are mobilized and articulated in influential film texts and the impact that these texts have had on popular culture at large.
Series Editors: Siân Lincoln and Yannis Tzioumakis

Titles in the series include:

Mustang
Translating Willful Youth
Elif Akçalı, Cüneyt Çakırlar, Özlem Güçlü

Mary Poppins
Radical Elevation in the 1960s
Leslie H. Abramson

The Outsiders
Adolescent Tenderness and Staying Gold
Ann M. Ciasullo

For a full list of titles and more information about this series, please visit: https://www.routledge.com/Cinema-and-Youth-Cultures/book-series/CYC

Mary Poppins
Radical Elevation in the 1960s

Leslie H. Abramson

Routledge
Taylor & Francis Group

LONDON AND NEW YORK

First published 2023
by Routledge
4 Park Square, Milton Park, Abingdon, Oxon OX14 4RN

and by Routledge
605 Third Avenue, New York, NY 10158

Routledge is an imprint of the Taylor & Francis Group, an informa business

© 2023 Leslie H. Abramson

British Library Cataloguing-in-Publication Data
A catalogue record for this book is available from the British Library

ISBN: 978-1-138-58640-6 (hbk)
ISBN: 978-1-032-43647-0 (pbk)
ISBN: 978-0-429-50460-0 (ebk)

DOI: 10.4324/9780429504600

Typeset in Times New Roman
by Deanta Global Publishing Services, Chennai, India

For my sons, Benjamin and Gabriel, and for Arthur,
with my most buoyant affection

Contents

Figures

Series Editors' Introduction

Despite the high visibility of youth films in the global media marketplace, especially since the 1980s when Conglomerate Hollywood realized that such films were not only strong box office performers but also the starting point for ancillary sales in other media markets as well as for franchise building, academic studies that focused specifically on such films were slow to materialize. Arguably the most important factor behind academia's reluctance to engage with youth films was a (then) widespread perception within the Film and Media Studies communities that such films held little cultural value and significance, and therefore were not worthy of serious scholarly research and examination. Just like the young subjects they represented, whose interests and cultural practices have been routinely deemed transitional and transitory, so were the films that represented them perceived as fleeting and easily digestible, destined to be forgotten quickly, as soon as the next youth film arrived in cinema screens a week later.

Under these circumstances, and despite a small number of pioneering studies in the 1980s and early 1990s, the field of 'youth film studies' did not really start blossoming and attracting significant scholarly attention until the 2000s and in combination with similar developments in cognate areas such as 'girl studies.' However, because of the paucity of material in the previous decades, the majority of these new studies in the 2000s focused primarily on charting the field and therefore steered clear of long, in-depth examinations of youth films or was exemplified by edited collections that chose particular films to highlight certain issues to the detriment of others. In other words, despite providing often wonderfully rich accounts of youth cultures as these have been captured by key films, these studies could not have possibly dedicate sufficient space to engage with more than just a few key aspects of youth films.

In more recent (post-2010) years a number of academic studies started delimiting their focus and therefore providing more space for in-depth examinations of key types of youth films, such as slasher films and biker films or examining youth films in particular historical periods. From that point on, it was a matter of time for the first publications that focused exclusively on key youth films from a number of perspectives to appear (*Mamma Mia! The Movie*, *Twilight* and *Dirty Dancing* are among the first films to receive this treatment). Conceived primarily as edited collections, these studies provided a multifaceted analysis of these films, focusing on such issues as the politics of representing youth, the stylistic and narrative choices that characterize these films and the extent to which they are representative of a youth cinema, the ways these films address their audiences, the ways youth audiences engage with these films, the films' industrial location and other relevant issues.

It is within this increasingly maturing and expanding academic environment that the **Cinema and Youth Cultures** volumes arrive, aiming to consolidate existing knowledge, provide new perspectives, apply innovative methodological approaches, offer sustained and in-depth analyses of key films and therefore become the 'go to' resource for students and scholars interested in theoretically informed, authoritative accounts of youth cultures in film. As editors, we have tried to be as inclusive as possible in our selection of key examples of youth films by commissioning volumes on films that span the history of cinema, including the silent film era; that portray contemporary youth cultures as well as ones associated with particular historical periods; that represent examples of mainstream and independent cinema; that originate in American cinema and the cinemas of other nations; that attracted significant critical attention and commercial success during their initial release and that were 'rediscovered' after an unpromising initial critical reception. Together these volumes are going to advance youth film studies while also being able to offer extremely detailed examinations of films that are now considered significant contributions to cinema and our cultural life more broadly.

We hope readers will enjoy the series.

Siân Lincoln & Yannis Tzioumakis
Cinema & Youth Cultures Series Editors

Acknowledgments

When my son Benjamin was a small boy, he became temporarily captivated by *Mary Poppins*. As I listened to the VHS tape playing repeatedly, I began to realize that this was a very different musical than that which I recalled from my early girlhood. Viewed through the lens of a film scholar, what came into focus were *Poppins'* many connections to its time. As I developed and taught courses on American cinema in the 1950s and 1960s, *Poppins* was a mainstay, and my students invariably responded with their own delight to regarding the film in its mid-century context.

Many thanks to my editors, Yannis Tzioumakis and Siân Lincoln, for their eagle-eyed readings, helpful suggestions, and patience. Everlasting gratitude is due to my original mentor at the University of Chicago, the late Gerald Mast, and many thanks to the late Miriam Hansen. My deepest love and appreciation go to my husband, Arthur, and my sons, Gabriel and Benjamin, wellsprings of constant love and support. Profound gratitude and love always to my mother and late father, Bernice and Leonard, and to my wonderful late grandmother, Sadie Glantz.

Introduction

Among the explosion of baby boomer films that rocked the 1960s, the most stirring early work was likely *Mary Poppins*. This 1964 film proved so captivating to young audiences that by the end of the following year *Poppins* (Stevenson) not only led *Variety*'s annual list of highest grossing domestic films but assumed fourth place in its tabulation of 'All-Time Top Grossers' behind the historical epics *Gone with the Wind* (Fleming, 1939), *Ben-Hur* (Wyler, 1959), and *The Ten Commandments* (DeMille, 1956) ('Big Rental ...' 1966; 'All-Time ...' 1966). The revenue that earned *Poppins* this spot was garnered from both first-time and storied repeat viewings. No less a director of defining 1960s cinema than Stanley Kubrick, whose *Dr. Strangelove: Or How I Learned to Stop Worrying and Love the Bomb* was *Poppins*' contemporary, recounted shortly after the release of *2001: A Space Odyssey* (1968), 'I saw *Mary Poppins* three times, because of my children, and I like Julie Andrews so much that I enjoyed seeing it three times. I thought that it was a charming film' (quoted in Kohler 1968: 86). The Disney musical was considered such a critical cultural experience that schoolchildren in the suburbs of Boston were bussed to screenings and youths bragged about how many times they had viewed the film. Capitalizing on this phenomenon, *Poppins* posters encouraged, 'See It Again and Again!'

Mary Poppins was duly embraced with enthusiasm by the popular entertainment industry, whose institutions presented it with their highest honors. Amply rewarded by Hollywood, *Poppins* won five Oscars. At the Grammys, *Poppins*' soundtrack outperformed the Beatles' *A Hard Day's Night* (Lester, 1964) for best original film score, and the record was *Billboard*'s Album of the Year in 1965. The Writers Guild of America named *Poppins* the 'Best Written Musical' of the year. Yet, contrary to *Poppins*' acclaim as an exemplar of classic children's cinema, its sensibility was more akin to Kubrick's and the Beatles' films, and it proved more of an almost cultish draw for its own young audiences. Viewed through the lens of the historical moment,

DOI: 10.4324/9780429504600-1

this film typically considered a timeless, antiseptic youth fantasy constitutes, rather, a work of distinct timeliness, an emphatically—albeit, among its complexities, not unequivocally—antiestablishment musical.

Poppins' attractions exceeded Disney's traditional high production values, its largely 'cheery disposition,' charismatic performances by leads Julie Andrews and Dick Van Dyke, and rousing music that together earned the film Academy Awards for Best Actress, Best Music (Original Score and Original Song), Best Special Visual Effects, and Best Film Editing, among 13 nominations that included one for Best Picture.[1] Read against the dominant grain of its reputation as a classically innocent youth film, *Poppins* registers as a feature highly determined by and invested in the radically changing times. This Disney release is rife with often unexplored allures as a musical teeming with the contemporary preoccupations of America's younger generation turbulently grappling with the ailments of the Establishment's prevailing order. Reflecting its context of the early-to-mid-1960s, *Poppins* is in essence a composition of modernity, a theater of countercultural unrest, anxieties, desires, and magical pleasures staged at a juncture of dramatic social turmoil.

In the course of its nearly two-and-a-half-hour runtime, *Poppins* unpacks a carpetbag of issues critical to the new decade. Set in London during 1910, *Poppins* is an Edwardian-shrouded display of cultural maladies, imperatives, and fantasies, costuming what was at stake for the troubled American young in the disquieted early 1960s. The film showcases contemporary cultural, social, political, and economic concerns through highly resonant narrative conditions and tensions: the dysfunctional nuclear family, the generation gap, youth unrest, the tyranny of capitalist imperialism, feminism and other antiestablishment activism, liberation discourses, socially conscious music, race relations, masculine gender anxieties, domestic and foreign affairs relevant to the Cold War and early Vietnam War years, and drug culture. When understood as a film strongly produced by its historical period, cinema both informed by and in effect addressing the position of baby boomers corseted in patriarchal culture, the abundantly well-received *Poppins* comes into focus as a musical that essentially stages antiestablishment values as remedies for a multitude of cross-generational ills.

At the same time, *Poppins* adheres to certain formal institutional obligations. Beholden to studio cinema's own economic and cultural order, the film is not an entirely unmitigated critique of the Establishment. Rather, for the consumption of mass family audiences, this 1964 Disneyfication of the exigencies of children's lives dually elevates and sanitizes figures and values representing radical change. Consequently, Disney's production constitutes a significant case of how, echoing mid-twentieth-century American cultural tumult, the mainstream Hollywood baby boomer film took the form of oppositional cinema while negotiating the shoals of commercialism. On continual display not only on screen but in the process of its creation, exhibition, and reception are authorial struggles among privileging liberation and alternativism, upholding the mandated economies of an entrenched production system, and contravening the extent to which the genre definition of children's cinema presumes to crystallize and limit both spectatorship and cultural impact.

Poppins' Genealogy: In Brief

Mary Poppins was the progeny of multiple authors with diverse ties to youth culture. The film originated from author P.L. Travers' 1934 book about a mystical nanny with phantasmagoric powers. This work proved so popular that the author serialized Poppins' adventures in a total of seven books, the last of which was published in 1988. As will be discussed in Chapter 2, Travers—who had theretofore made her living as a journalist and wrote fiction and poetry for adult audiences—became a celebrated children's author, a designation that she resisted together with the widespread perception that *Poppins* was solely literature for youths. Throughout the rest of her life, she would continually attempt to liberate so-called children's fantasy from mainstream definitions of the genre and its audience. Nonetheless, under Disney's supervision and as recomposed through the lens of the early 1960s, Travers' Mary would speak compellingly to baby boomers. In addition to particular familial and economic anxieties of the original *Poppins*' Depression-set London adapted to Disney's Edwardian-era film—facets that, as magnified on screen, resonate with 1960s cultural concerns—*Poppins* is informed by its author's own alternative sensibility, including her early engrossment with Eastern spirituality and other interests to which youths were drawn at the time that Mary reached the cinema.

The transformation of Travers' *Poppins* into a Disney musical entailed harmonizing multiple authorial voices from the studio. Central to the adaptation were the conventions and codes of Disney cinema, tendencies of Disney mid-twentieth-century films, mandates of commercialism, and Walt Disney's midcentury cultural and political concerns. These were joined by the sensibilities of, most notably, Robert and Richard Sherman, the musical's composers and contributing writers, who were allied with teen culture as creators of pop music. Working within the powerfully determinative context of the historical moment, *Poppins*' diverse producers—to be discussed in forthcoming chapters—collectively formulated a portrait of youths' domestic conditions and imperatives that spoke evocatively to young baby boomers. Yet, even the Disney team did not constitute the final word on *Mary Poppins*. Upon its theatrical release, *Poppins* continued to be recast, this time through domains of contemporary reception. Ultimately liberated from Disney, the film was not only generally acclaimed and assimilated into mid-twentieth-century cultural lexicons but produced various cultural tensions, thereby becoming its own contested and contrarian text.

From the original volume's identification as a story that defied entrenched conceptions about child-centered narratives, through the musical's reception, *Poppins* bespoke how youth fantasies could address adult audiences. Dating from Travers' early pronouncements, supported by enchanted readers and book critics (see Chapter 3), and greatly amplified upon the film's release, *Poppins* became a phenomenon that broadened the definition, audience, and cultural influence of so-called juvenile works. As will be explored in Chapter 6, Disney's *Poppins* became the rage figuratively and literally through its wide cultural embrace and simultaneous provocation of controversy among those dedicated to maintaining traditional order. The film's verbal and harmonic vocabulary was adopted extensively, entering the popular lexicon as well as music ranging from easy listening tunes to jazz and rock. *Poppins* songs were recorded by vocalists from long-established crooners to those who would become known for antiwar protest songs, in various respects conveying timely messages during a period of escalating turmoil. Albeit recognized as an iconic production, *Poppins* was appropriated not only for the purposes of the prevailing bourgeois sensibility but also for those of the counterculture. The film became notoriously construed by some older youths as a trippy experience, an interpretation cheekily approved of by its star, who would disavow her saccharine Disney image. In such regards, the film become a site of tension between mainstream and alternative orientations.

Poppins' contributions to popular culture were not without additional controversy. As will also be discussed in Chapter 6, some strongly criticized the film for corrupting youth by degrading classic children's fiction. A vocal contingent judged Disney's *Poppins* a poor, syrupy adaptation whose cultural violations were compounded by even more distortive product tie-ins, altogether amounting to vulgar commercial imperialism. Consequently, within the dialectics of authorship this youth film continually grappled with conflicts between celebrating rebellion against the Establishment and contravening its values by submitting to Disney's own institutional capitalist obligations.

Poppins further exhibited its association with midcentury cultural concerns and preoccupations through an affinity with a recently emerged film genre, the teenpic. Just as the literary *Poppins* was identified as a fantasy that spanned genre definitions, so, too, did Disney's adaptation inherently challenge categorical youth film divisions. In another unexplored facet to be discussed in Chapter 6, *Poppins* is akin to teenpics in certain important respects. Among these, through *Poppins'* youth-associated music, archaic mainstream culture becomes resuscitated—an enterprise that allies Disney's release with some key teen musicals from the 1950s to the Beatles' *A Hard Day's Night*. Moving beyond such kindred approaches, *Poppins* contributed not only to the early idealism of youth activism and the perceived potential of social revolution, but also to a darkly complicated view of the future. The film advanced the spirit of youth antiestablishmentarianism while constituting a cautionary tale. *Poppins'* storied uplifting conclusion is shaded by forewarnings that expose the vision of truly transformative rebellion embraced by all generations as yet another form of illusion.

Taken together, the pages to follow constitute a new journey through *Poppins*. The forthcoming chapters explore the film's significantly influential historical context, trace the formulation of Travers' literary fantasy and Disney's screen adaptation, closely analyze the musical, and examine its multifaceted reception. The considerations of Travers and Disney (Chapters 2 and 3) key on how certain philosophies, values, and preoccupations imbuing the creators' works chimed with (and, in Disney's case, also collided with) particular burgeoning concerns and antiestablishment sensibilities of the 1960s vital to the film. A two-part analysis of *Poppins* (Chapters 4 and 5) unpacks the musical's timely anxieties, ideals, and struggles between remedially liberating countercultural experience and the reigning power structure constantly threatening its foreclosure. The final chapter examines *Poppins'* reception as an inspiring yet contested film, in various regards itself a battleground upon which the decade's conflicts, radicalisms, and inspirations materialized as youth cinema emphatically took its place as a potent cultural force screening revolutionary, yet problematized, visions.

Note

1 The film's Oscar nominations included those for Directing, Art Direction, Cinematography, and Writing (best adapted screenplay).

1   Step in Time: *Poppins* and the 1960s

Mary Poppins arrived on screen during a moment of increasing domestic turbulence. When the musical premiered, on 27 August 1964 at the iconic Grauman's Chinese Theatre in Los Angeles, an enthused celebrity interviewer, recognizing the gala as the veneer of another cheerier yesteryear, rhapsodized, 'it makes Hollywood seem like Hollywood of the old days again' ('The World Premiere ...' 2016). Not only did the gleeful, tuxedo- and gown-bedecked red carpet entrances belie a perished studio system but an American culture in the throes of growing unrest, upheaval, and division. Accomplishing the 'job that must be done' with 'A Spoonful of Sugar,' according to Disney's ethos, the musical buoyantly showcased to young baby boomers an aggregate of generational tensions, disaffections, fantasies, inclinations toward escapism, and antiestablishment rebellion not unfamiliar to those living outside the diegetic confines of Cherry Tree Lane.

Poppins emerged from, and in turn contributed to, the cultural conversation at a time of proliferating youth discontent, protest, activism for social change, new alternative lifestyles, and captivation with transcendent, consciousness-expanding experiences. So, too, was much of the film imbued with optimism about the possibilities of youth resistance and counterculturalism, a sentiment particularly in tune with the decade's early hopefulness about the potential for ameliorating the ills of the parochial dominant order. Although, to be discussed in Chapter 3 and as asserted by Douglas Brode in *From Walt to Woodstock* (2004), it was not wholly out of character for a Disney film of the time to espouse certain countercultural values, *Poppins* is strongly shaped by its historical context insofar as it bespeaks many youth-associated concerns and attitudes of the 1960s.

The period of *Poppins'* production and reception was one of dramatic national and international escalations. In the early-to-mid-1960s, the domestic strife of the generation gap, civil rights activism, growing feminist advocacy, antinuclear weapon protests, and allied student antiestablishment

DOI: 10.4324/9780429504600-2

protest movements on American soil, together with U.S. entanglement in conflicts beyond its borders, roiled the nation. The decade began with a celebration of a youthful universal vision. With the 1960 election of John F. Kennedy, the youngest president voted into office, the idealism of youth's promise emanated in part from the White House, as did an optimistic agenda of social change termed the New Frontier[1]—only to suffer a catastrophic blow in 1963 with his traumatic assassination. In its tragic wake, activism (student-fueled and otherwise) continued to proliferate, as did progressive domestic policy when in 1964 Kennedy's successor, Lyndon Johnson, began to pursue an agenda of liberal social reforms through his Great Society programs. At the same time, the U.S. was in the throes of one international conflict and on the threshold of another as the Cold War continued to rage and the Vietnam War was just beginning to ramp up to a full-scale, increasingly broadcast military struggle costing ever-mounting numbers of lives.

Central among the rifts cleaving the domestic cultures of the U.S. and *Poppins* during the 1960s was a widespread concern termed 'the generation gap.' This fissure within the venerated bedrock of the nuclear family emerged in youth cinema as a deeply troubling development with the advent of the teenpic in the mid-1950s. During the film's prehistory, troubled youths of the post-WWII decades were the subject of much-publicized concern among sociologists, psychologists, educators, parents, politicians, and civic leaders, who produced widely disseminated books, articles, and studies. The Senate Judiciary Subcommittee to Investigate Juvenile Delinquency was formed in 1954 and held hearings for the next ten years. The struggles of youths and the attendant adult cultural anxieties exploded onto the screen with *The Wild One* (Benedek, 1953), *Blackboard Jungle* (Brooks, 1955), and *Rebel Without a Cause* (Ray, 1955), teen social problem films for general audiences that proved highly popular with young viewers. Thomas Doherty observes that *Blackboard Jungle*, a gritty film about a New York inner city school, 'remains a harsh testimony to how wide the gulf between parents and teenagers had become by the mid-1950s. [...] Throughout [the film] was a real sense that the terms of the social contract between young and old had changed' (2002: 58). Alternately, *Rebel*, which takes place in the well-manicured Los Angeles suburbs, scrutinizes the domestic rift resulting in youths' delinquency as a consequence not of economically impoverished upbringings but rather of an environment in which empty middle class materialist values supplant parental support and understanding. This condition was engendered by parents' emotional and physical absence from their children's lives. Pointing to how these initial genre films address parent–child strife and the culpability of the older generation, Jon Mitchell notes, 'the ideal of the stable nuclear family unit [is] silently held in high esteem in *Rebel*. The film [...] shows the problems that occur when this unit becomes deficient and dysfunctional' (2005: 136). He cites Peter Biskind's observation that 'it quickly becomes evident that it is not [the teenagers] who are the delinquents but their parents' (quoted in ibid.). In other words, cinema undertook a culturally diagnostic role with regard to the troubles of youth, specifically focusing on domestic issues.

The rupture and discord that triggered James Dean's resonant wail to his parents in *Rebel Without a Cause*, 'You're tearing me apart!' and later vexed the fractured Banks family, were diagnosed as a growing cultural issue in the mid-twentieth century. William Whyte's 1956 book, *The Organization Man*, paints a bleak portrait of patriarchs who in the decade to follow would be characterized as members of the Establishment: 'the ones of our middle class who have left home, spiritually as well as physically, to take the vows of organization life' (2002: 3). Whyte identifies this problematic condition, typified on screen by the all-too-committed employee of the Fidelity Fiduciary Bank, as particularly significant in America insofar as conformism contravenes the founding tenets of 'personal independence and freedom' (5). The book, a bestseller, was of such contemporary relevance that it was reprinted in 1957, 1959, 1960, 1963, 1965, 1967, and 1969. In a 1960 book initially commissioned as an examination of juvenile delinquency, the best-selling *Growing Up Absurd*, Paul Goodman explores the 'disaffection of the growing generation' (2012: 5) with the 'frivolous racket' of modern capitalist corporate culture (39). Explaining the motivation for his project, Goodman notes that a book had yet to be published on 'Youth Problems in the Organized System' (ibid.). This system, writes Goodman, 'muffles the voices of dissent; and then it irrefutably proclaims that itself is the only possibility of society, for nothing else is thinkable' (6). Goodman asserts that in order to combat the situation, 'radical changes' are required (9) and stresses historical precedents: 'In outrageously bad ages [...] rebellious youth is esteemed as the hoped-for agent of change. These attitudes all make sense and apply in our times too' (213).

In the 1960s, 'generation gap' was a popular diagnostic term, one closely associated with concerns about the dysfunctional family. Addressing such issues in a 1962 newspaper article, 'Generation Gap Affects Parent–Child Relations,' Barnard College president Millicent McIntosh dispensed advice (paraphrased by a reporter) as relevant to *Poppins*' George and Winifred Banks as to the parents of baby boomers:

> To handle [youth rebellion] best, she suggests that a parent stand by, ready to sympathize and to discuss problems, rather than just assert authority. [...] Sufficient support and love on the part of parents—no matter how busy you are running your own life and your home—are

essential as an antidote to this. [...] 'Share your young people's world altogether,' she urges.

(Roesch 1962: 6)

In a 1962 issue of the academic journal *Daedalus*, titled 'Youth: Change and Challenge,' child psychologist Bruno Bettelheim's essay 'The Problem of Generations' explores yet other worries associated with the contemporary nuclear family. Bettelheim describes how generational conflict results from modern conditions in which parents are more strongly invested in their children's conformity to the older generation's lifestyle than their progeny's independence (Bettelheim 1962: 72).[2] Discussing troubles that *Poppins* viewers would recognize as characteristic of George Banks and his offspring, Bettelheim identifies a facet 'of the conflict of generations: the parent who sees his child's main task in life as the duty to execute his [(the former's)] will or to justify his existence' (74). By the end of the decade, screen images of the generation gap would reach an apotheosis with the top-grossing cynical cultural portrait *The Graduate* (Nichols, 1967). Underscoring the accordant commercial possibilities for the film industry, a *Variety* writer asserted, '*The Graduate* spanned the generation gap, and Joe Levine [president of its production company, Avco-Embassy Pictures] has the profits to prove it' (Pryor 1968: 10).

Summing up the youth zeitgeist on 1 October 1964 at a University of California, Berkeley free speech rally, arrested student activist Jack Weinberg declared to a reporter, 'We have a saying in the movement that we don't trust anyone over 30' (Pogash 2014: A18). Asserted the same day that *Poppins* star Julie Andrews turned 29, the expression encapsulated the spirit of generational rebellion coupled with the idealistic stirrings of social revolution emergent from the turn of the decade. In *The Sixties: Years of Hope, Days of Rage*, Todd Gitlin observes, 'From social tensions came a tumult of movements aiming to remake virtually every social arrangement America had settled into after World War II' (1993: 5). The burgeoning political, social, and cultural movements were energetically (although not singularly) fueled by the younger generation. In 1960, the 'new left' activist group, Students for a Democratic Society (SDS), was formed. Two years later, the SDS issued the influential *Port Huron Statement*, a manifesto for youth-mobilized political and social change that called for 'participatory democracy,' denounced imperialism and capitalism, and advocated civil disobedience (Students for a Democratic Society 1962). Distinguishing a significant divide between the young and their elders, the manifesto begins with an 'Agenda for a Generation' stating, 'We are people of this generation, bred in at least moderate comfort [...] looking uncomfortably to the world we inherit' (ibid.) The manifesto's mandates include enlisting youth in the cause: 'A new left must consist of younger people who matured in the postwar world, and partially be directed to the recruitment of younger people' (ibid.).[3] Displaying its cinematic attunement to the spirit of the moment, *Poppins* is in various regards infused with similar perspectives.

By the time that Mary Poppins arrived on screen to inspire and provide direction to the rebellious, tactfully outspoken Banks children by defying the patriarchal order and its capitalist imperialism, outside movie theaters oppositional movements and the struggle for participatory democracy were ramping up among youths and others advancing the cause of social revolution. Tom Hayden, who drafted the *Port Huron Statement*, was inspired by the work of the Student Nonviolent Coordinating Committee (SNCC), a civil rights protest group that emerged in 1960 and actively advocated for desegregation in the South. In the wake of growing protests calling for racial equality in the 1950s, civil rights activism in the new decade increasingly became part of the landscape of antiestablishment resistance, and its struggles ever-more-widely transmitted via moving images. The activism of Black college students' 1960 sit-in at a Whites-only lunch counter in Greensboro, North Carolina, the SNCC's 1961 interracial Freedom Rides challenging noncompliance with federal desegregation laws and voter registration drives,[4] the 1963 March on Washington for Jobs and Freedom culminating with Martin Luther King, Jr.'s' 'I Have a Dream' speech delivered before an estimated 250,000 gathered at the Lincoln Memorial—together with many other marches, protests, and demonstrations of civil disobedience often met with violently racist opposition—constituted striking footage broadcast with progressive frequency on American televisions. When *Poppins*' marginalized smudge-faced and black-clad chimney sweeps took the screen for the production number 'Step in Time,' essentially a complicated, problematic display of antiracism, the government had begun to address discrimination through the transformative Civil Rights Acts of 1957, 1960, and 1964.

Referencing the film in association with another of the decade's conflicts, one raging abroad and at home, a 1968 *New Yorker* cartoon pictured a middle-aged man conservatively dressed in suit and tie, remarking to his wife, 'Frankly, I don't see any point in continuing a discussion of our position in Southeast Asia with someone who went to see "Mary Poppins" three times' (Darrow 1968: 36) [see Figure 1.1]. Exhibiting chauvinism typical of George Banks, the husband dismisses the female independent voice and defiant sensibility. By implication deriding the antiwar sentiment held by an admirer of the pacifistic *Poppins* and conjunctively firing a broadside against an aficionada of mass culture whose tastes are not restricted by classic genre delineations of children's fantasy, the bespectacled husband displays a myopic militarism akin to that of Admiral Boom. The wife's

"*Frankly, I don't see any point in continuing a discussion of our position in Southeast Asia with someone who went to see 'Mary Poppins' three times.*"

Figure 1.1 New Yorker cartoon, 1968 (Whitney Darrow, Jr.)

cited outspokenness signals sympathy with not only the extensive antimilitary movement but a crusade echoing that of the film's committed suffragette Mrs. Banks, who also struggles on the domestic front. By the time of *Poppins'* release, midcentury feminist activism had been gathering momentum. Feminist voices became progressively loud from the outset of the decade when, as Anna Everett notes, 'new revelations about women's dissatisfaction with prevailing sexual attitudes and gender expectations could no longer be contained' (2008: 46). In 1960, women's widespread sexual liberation was initiated with the introduction of the first oral contraceptive, 'The Pill.' In a magazine article published that same year, Margaret Mead considered, 'What Makes Women Unhappy?' (1960). The following year, Kennedy established the President's Commission on the Status of Women. His Executive Order states at the outset: 'prejudices and outmoded customs act as barriers to the full realization of women's basic rights which should be respected and fostered as part of our Nation's commitment to human dignity, freedom, and democracy' (President's ... 1963: 76). The Commission's study, issued in 1963, commenced with the mandate, 'This report is an invitation to action' (1). In February 1963, exposing the oppressive mythology of women's fulfillment in homemaking, Betty Friedan published *The Feminine Mystique*. This revolutionary best-selling book, excerpts of which appeared in the popular magazines *Ladies' Home Journal* and *McCall's*, played a key role in galvanizing what became known as the second-wave feminist movement, following first-wave suffragettism of the late 1800s–early 1900s that was Winifred Banks' cause.[5]

Militarisms

At the beginning of the decade, considerable female militancy took the form of antiwar protests, displaying another burgeoning, youth-focused cultural concern that constituted the backdrop of *Poppins'* production and reception. Women's activism was, in part, devoted to protesting Cold War policies and the Vietnam War—anxieties resonant in the film's troubling vision of martial imperialism. In 1961, the year that President Kennedy called up 120,000 Army reservists to active duty (Stewart 2010: 298), approximately 50,000 women in 60 cities across the U.S. staged a day-long strike advocating nuclear disarmament. The organization formed through coordinating this protest against policies and conditions endangering children, Women Strike for Peace would 'In early 1964 [become] among the first to oppose the Vietnam War,' as noted by Rebecca Solnit in *The Nation* (2006). At the time, the U.S. was becoming mired in a war that was increasingly prominent in public discourse and images. By the end of 1959, the U.S. military had suffered its first casualties from North Vietnam forces. In 1962, approximately 11,000 American 'military advisors' were aiding the South Vietnamese; the number of military personnel would escalate to 16,000 in 1963 and 24,000 the following year (Military n.d., Stewart 2010: 301). As the war intensified through the early 1960s, so did media coverage of the conflict's neocolonialist facets, its intransigencies, the bombast of military pronouncements camouflaging a lost cause—all, in effect, destabilizing blind shots across the bow of domestic culture—and international relations.

Discomfiting public images and expressions of dissatisfaction with the war were not unknown in the early 1960s. In June 1963, a news photo published globally showed a monk setting himself on fire in protest against South Vietnam's brutally repressive American-backed regime. In a September 1963 nationally broadcast interview, President Kennedy—who commented, 'No news picture in history has generated so much emotion around the world as that one'—discussed the war with CBS News' Walter Cronkite, America's most-trusted anchor. Cronkite observed, 'the only hot war we've got running […] is, of course, the one on Vietnam. And we've got our difficulties there.' Kennedy replied,

> I don't think that unless a greater effort is made by the government to win popular support that the war can be won out there. […] I don't agree with those who say we should withdraw. That would be a great mistake. I know people don't like Americans to be engaged in this kind of an effort.
>
> (Kennedy 1963)

Ratcheting up the war during the months leading to *Poppins*' release, the Gulf of Tonkin incident, an early August 1964 confrontation between North Vietnamese and U.S. ships, resulted in a resolution authorizing President Johnson to 'take all necessary measures to repel any armed attack against the forces of the United States and to prevent further aggression' by the North Vietnamese (Tonkin 1964).

Although student anti-Vietnam War protests began the year following *Poppins*' release, prior to 1964 the younger generation prominently staged Cold War-associated peace demonstrations throughout the country. Among these, the National Committee for a Sane Nuclear Policy (SANE), established in 1957, generated student chapters across college campuses and was joined by numerous film stars. In 1960, a SANE rally at Madison Square Garden attracted a crowd of an estimated 20,000 (Swerdlow 1993: 45) protesting nuclear testing and advocating nuclear disarmament—only to witness the near-realization of their worst fears two years later during the Cuban Missile Crisis, a standoff between U.S. Navy and Russian vessels that brought the countries to the brink of war. In the early 1960s, antiwar activism was also ramping up through the public statements of such prominent figures as SANE co-chair Dr. Benjamin Spock, author of the best-selling book on parenting, *The Common Sense Book of Baby and Child Care* (originally published in 1946, the outset of the baby boom). In a 1962 *Life* magazine article, Spock,

who would become famed that decade as an antiwar and nuclear disarmament activist, asserted, 'There's no point in raising children if they're going
to be burned alive' ('Quick, Go Get …' 1962: 92).[6] Accordingly, during a
moment of heightened American cultural imperialism, reformers brought an
investment in youths' wellbeing to the forefront of public concerns.

During the early-to-mid-1960s, in concert with those challenging the prevailing order through protest rallies, demonstrations, manifestos, pamphlets,
books of social criticism, and mass media interviews, arose a chorus of folk
singers. The cultural moment of *Poppins*' production and exhibition was
one increasingly suffused with songs of social consciousness and rebellion.
Bert's one-man concert in the park, punctuated by his rhyming discernment
of shifting winds, was performed shortly following the emergence of the
most powerful antiestablishment musical voice of the 1960s, Bob Dylan,
who poetically vocalized changes in the air in his 1962 song, 'Blowin' in
the Wind.' The song would soon become a peace and civil rights anthem,
performed by folk group Peter, Paul, and Mary in advance of King's 'I
Have a Dream' speech at the 1963 March on Washington. The group's first
album, released in 1962, included such allegorical protest songs (what Todd
Gitlin terms 'political song-parables' [1993: 75]) as 'Where Have All the
Flowers Gone' and 'If I Had a Hammer,' written by folk singer and social
activist Pete Seeger. Together with the revival of such songs as Seeger's
'Turn! Turn! Turn!' adapted from Ecclesiastes in 1959 and first recorded by
others for popular release in 1962 and 1963, the refashioning of traditional
(sometimes spiritual) lyrics and music for protest and advocating an idealistic, prescriptive vision of reform was burgeoning. The adapted harmonies
of some of these songs anticipate such *Poppins* numbers as 'Feed the Birds.'

The genre of the film musical itself, as well as the scoring of nonmusicals,
was undergoing a transformation with which *Poppins* was in certain regards
allied. Paul Monaco notes, 'The 1960s was a decade in which the types of
music that might acceptably accompany feature films changed entirely'
(2001: 109). The decade began with the 1961 release of the socially conscious,
amply budgeted musicals *West Side Story* (Wise and Robbins) and *Flower
Drum Song* (Koster) (one a work of gritty realism and the other a standard
studio production), initiating the trend of what Anna Everett describes as
'a range of Hollywood and independent film productions exploring topical
issues of the period' (2008: 48). Both are interracial romances that center
on issues of youths oppressed by intolerance coupled with the intransigencies of the generation gap—and, as a result, critically in need of acceptance,
understanding, and liberation from the status quo. In the consequent stylistic
fissure between such top-grossing young generation musicals as 1964's *A
Hard Day's Night* and *Poppins*, the *cinéma vérité* graphics and rock 'n' roll
music of the former, although divergent from the seeming conventionality of

the latter, do not reflect an incongruous cultural perspective. In fact, of the two immensely popular, outspokenly antiestablishment youth musicals set in England, *Poppins* more specifically addresses the condition, stresses, and fantasies of the young grappling with patriarchal mainstream culture.

Escapism

Amidst the decade's growing turbulence, during which *Poppins'* escapist fantasies proved so captivating, youth were increasingly drawn to chemically and spiritually altered states of consciousness. Inspired by prominent countercultural figures, the younger generation pursued the emancipatory, mind-expanding enchantments of drugs, nonconformist lifestyles, and the spirituality of Eastern religions. Proliferating from the renowned drug use of such 1950s Beat Generation writers as Allen Ginsburg and Jack Kerouac, and Harvard lecturer Timothy Leary's publicized LSD experiments on himself and students from 1960 to 1962, not only did the use of marijuana and psychedelics mushroom but drug culture would exert an increasing impact on popular music as well as cinema aesthetics. Also rooted in the Beat movement, the rise of Zen Buddhism, Hinduism, and Hindu-based transcendental meditation rose in the 1960s among those, as Camille Paglia writes, 'seeking the truth about life outside religious and social institutions' (2003: 58). Such enchantment was quite familiar to P.L. Travers beginning in the 1920s, when she was introduced to Eastern spiritualities to which she would be dedicated for the rest of her life. With the popularity of mysticism, together with the vision of the space race and the specter of nuclear destruction, Paglia observes, 'The sixties generation [...] had been injected with a mystical sense of awe and doom about the sky' (95)—an environment into which Disney's *Poppins* lands. Together, these lineages, predating and constituting the distinct cultural context of the early-to-mid-1960s, converged to contribute to the enchantment of *Poppins'* alternative vision.

  Poppins arrived in 1964 as a creation of and commentary on cultural forces that resonated well beyond what has generally been considered the circumscribed, saccharine nature of Disney youth cinema. Albeit attired in the habiliments of the Edwardian age, according to its own literal and allegorical discourse *Poppins* struggles with the new decade's here and now, grappling with contemporary dysfunctions of the patriarchal order, antiestablishment rebellion, and escapism at a time when baby boomers were increasingly asserting their oppositional voices. A complicated, conflicted film, *Poppins* manifests concurrently optimistic and jaded perspectives informed in part by its status as a studio genre production—beholden to the mandate of capitalism yet contemptuous of it, delineating a paternal domesticity that must be eluded yet longing for its celebration, and other tensions. Among the adaptation's construction, the musical's entangle- ments, and *Poppins'* striking reception lie documentation and document echoing the agitations and fantasies of the 1960s, a dialogue with the decade that magnetized contemporary audiences. *Poppins* transported to the screen uplifting mobilization and opposition, inspiration contesting nearly intran- sigent allegiance to the prevailing order, leading to revolutionary transfor- mation that is ultimately recontained. In other words, *Poppins* was uniquely attuned to the present, a scenario enacted for baby boomers that in essence indicated how the decade would play out, a trajectory of radical optimism which, concluding with the anticipated return of Poppins and other signs, forecasted the new idealism's eventual fall to earth.

Notes

1 Kennedy used the term in his acceptance speech at the 1960 Democratic National Convention.
2 So concerning were generational differences and struggles that other academic journals at the turn of the decade and throughout the 1960s also addressed the conditions of youths at length. *The Annals of the American Academy of Political and Social Science* published issues titled Prevention of Juvenile Delinquency (1959, including the essay 'Delinquency Prevention Through Revitalizing Parent–Child Relations'), Teen-Age Culture (1961), and Protest in the Sixties (1969).
3 The manifesto identifies university students as 'an obvious beginning point' in efforts to recruit the young.
4 The Freedom Riders were multiracial groups of civil rights activists who rode public buses into the South. The brutalities that they endured demonstrated how southern states repudiated federal laws prohibiting segregation on interstate buses.
5 In 1966, the seminal activist organization for women's rights, NOW (National Organization of Women) was established with Friedan as president.
6 Spock's book was both celebrated and criticized for prescribing permissive parenting.

2 Mary's Generation

P.L. Travers, Unorthodoxy, and the Character of Modernity

Despite her image of forbidding sternness and rigidity that crystallized in print and eventually became rendered in sharp focus on screen with *Poppins'* origin story, Disney's *Saving Mr. Banks* (Hancock, 2013), author P.L. Travers was remarkably unbound. Inclined to unconventional free-spiritedness, Travers was in many respects a nonconformist, a woman who liberated herself from traditional expectations regarding gender, lifestyle, occupation, spirituality, and, to a degree, literature. Among Travers' prolific writings, the *Poppins* books from which the film is drawn evince diverse elements of her cultural sensibility through resistance to and critique of the dominant order of Depression-era England, a fantasy largely constructed of youths' serial introductions to unorthodox experience and points of view that free them from rigid, unfulfilling quotidian existence. Celebrated as a 'modern classic' for decades after the original volume's 1934 publication, *Mary Poppins* indeed constituted a work of contemporaneity and timeless-ness, fiction whose antiestablishment defiance and elevating alternativism became a particularly fitting source text for baby boomer cinema.

Travers' broadly popular *Mary Poppins* was followed by seven more books on the magical nanny written over the course of 55 years. Together with the initial work, the second and third in the series, *Mary Poppins Comes Back* (1935) and *Mary Poppins Opens the Door* (1943), were sources of the fantasy that, recomposed through the lens of Disney cinema, defined the title character's midcentury public image. Much as the literary and screen *Poppins* came to define Travers as well, the nanny did not arrive unaccompanied. Travers' series was part of an oeuvre that spanned multiple genres and preoccupations. Over the course of a writing career that began in the early 1920s and ended in the 1990s, she was a journalist, drama critic, poet, travel writer, author of fiction, opinion piece columnist, and writer of essays on fairy tales, myth, and spiritualism.

The preface to a *Paris Review* interview with Travers astutely observed, 'There is something both mythic and modern about her' (Burness and

DOI: 10.4324/9780429504600-3

Griswold 1982: 212). A self-described antiauthoritarian, upon emigrating from Australia to England in 1924 Travers gravitated to an alternative cultural movement, the Irish Literary Renaissance, and in turn embraced its figures' dedication to nonmainstream spirituality, established unconventional domestic arrangements, and rebelled against prevailing notions of youth fiction. A devotee of myth and almost cultish adherent to Eastern spiritualism, Travers perceived all human experience and cultures as bound together through history and lore that bespoke an ongoing mythic search for meaning, and she considered every element of the natural world deeply connected. In the construction of *Poppins'* characters and their sociocultural milieu, Travers' unorthodox sensibility was manifest in her representations of the bankruptcy of the Establishment, the Otherness of youth within the patriarchal domestic order, the valorization of children's solidarity with nature, the power of female independence and tensions of its circumscription, a sense of cosmic oneness, and the liberation endowed by antiauthoritarianism and consciousness-expanding undertakings, among other concerns and interests to flower in the 1960s. Such nonconformist perspectives, together with additional liberalisms infusing tales of the British nanny, produced *Poppins* as a work that, as adapted by Disney, would explicitly and allegorically exhibit a countercultural point of view that appealed strongly to youths during the new decade.

Travers' Flights

The experience of counterbalancing harsh domestic economic, familial, and psychological realities with escapist visions of literature, oral tradition, and performance constituted a critical facet of the author's early life. Born Helen Lyndon Goff in 1899, she was the oldest child of a struggling banker. The family initially lived above the Australian Joint Stock Bank's Maryborough branch, which was managed by her father, Travers, whose name she would adopt. Despite the presumed security of her father's position, the stability of neither banking nor the conventional patriarchal family was guaranteed—a condition later to be reflected in the profession of *Poppins'* George Banks and the travails of his literary family. Not only had the institution temporarily closed in 1893 as part of a banking collapse during Australia's economic depression of the 1890s (associated with troubles in the English banking industry), but Travers Goff was an alcoholic who would lose and regain his managerial position in the course of transfers to multiple branches (Lawson 2013: 46, 29). His death when his eldest daughter was seven left the family in both emotional and financial straits. They were rescued from the latter by a stern, wealthy unmarried aunt, Ellie (Helen Morehead), identified by the author's biographer and others as a model for Poppins (21, 32).[1]

The adversities and instability of Travers' girlhood were not accompanied by privations of spirit. Introduced by her parents (particularly her father) and others to mythology, the constellations, fairy tales, legend, and the Irish literature of the Goffs' heritage, the young Travers led a rich and unbound imaginative life. A bookish youth given to storytelling and writing, by her own account Travers' sanctuary was the world of fantasy. Although born of difficult times, for this she credited her young home life. In Travers' account of her childhood, domestic formalities of the early 1900s dissociated parents and offspring in a way that was painful yet unfettering, resulting in the liberation essential to youths' self-actualization. In her 1965 *New York Times* (*NYT*) article 'A Radical Innocence,' Travers wrote,

> I am grateful now, though I wasn't then [...] that I grew up in an atmosphere in which tradition was still part of life [...] and children taken for granted; not 'understood' in our modern sense, not looked upon as a special race [...] In our family life it was [my parents'] moods that were to be respected, not ours. It was clear that they had their own existence—busy, contained, important. And this, as I now see, left us free for ours.
>
> (1965: 1)

Animating the *Poppins* books with a similar rift that spawned the younger generation's pursuit of alternative fulfillments, Travers serialized certain conditions that decades later would be diagnosed as symptoms of the dysfunctional family.

Albeit accorded a certain measure of release by her traditional upbringing in the British colony, Travers would applaud modern youths for a degree of liberation unobtainable during her childhood. In 1967, as the decade's countercultural rebellion neared its apex, she reflected in an interview,

> I think I most admire today's young people [...] The generation that is growing up [...] seem just wonderful. So full of life and so unafraid. I'm always hearing bad things about them and reading startling things in the newspapers, but when I meet them I always find that they are a new and beautiful race. [...] Children today are so much freer than I ever was.
>
> (Newquist 1967: 430–431)

An enthusiastic supporter of the young generation's spirited independence, Travers herself had led an increasingly liberated life during her early years. Single and self-supporting from young womanhood through her death at 96,

Travers defied traditional gender expectations and cultural conservatisms. During the author's youth, Caitlin Flanagan notes, 'If it was possible to be a rebellious teen-ager in the girls' schools of Sydney in the nineteen-tens, then Travers was one' (2005: 42). As a student at a private academy, Travers became enamored with drama, acting in (as well as writing about and directing) school productions. Upon graduating, she briefly bowed to family pressure to take on a secretarial job, which she soon abandoned for an acting career. In the early 1920s, Travers performed supporting roles in theater productions of Shakespeare and popular contemporary drama throughout Australia and New Zealand, in part traveling with a touring company whose members, according to her biographer, she found alluringly uninhibited and with whom (among others) she experienced an array of freedoms.

In 1923, Travers relinquished her turn at theatrics for an even more absorbing passion: writing. Her poetry, drama criticism, essays, short stories, and travelogues were published in popular and respected Australian and New Zealand news and arts periodicals, including *The Triad, The Bulletin, Christchurch Sun,* and *Shakespeare Quarterly.* The young Travers was not simply a contributor to these publications; they contributed to her work in varying regards by shaping (or at least sharpening) facets of her authorial sensibility. The arts journal *The Triad* defined its mandate as a challenge to orthodoxy. *The Triad* rejected '"all forms of intolerance,"' including 'puritanism [and] propriety,' an agenda that 'had its roots in 1890s bohemianism [and] still sound[ed] daringly modern in the new century,' observes David Carter (2018: 250). Accordingly, some of Travers' published romantic poems employed images of sexual liberation.[2] In other cases, Travers' early published writings were subject to restrictive gender delineations that circumscribed their genre and acceptance. Travers wrote the columns 'Pamela Passes' in the 'Women's World' section of the *Christchurch Sun* and 'A Woman Hits Back' for *The Triad*, the latter described by the editors as a 'pageful of candid feminism' (Lawson 2013: 70, 80; 'Pamela Travers' 1924: 36). Albeit wary of the feminist cause, she would later rebel against sexism in publishing and the reception of literature by modifying her authorial name to the gender-nonspecific 'P.L. Travers.' In a 1964 interview, she explained that in doing so she sought liberation from authorial stereotypes:

[Fiction considered] children's books [...] are usually thought to be associated with women. I was determined not to have this label of sentimentality put on me so I signed by my initials, hoping people wouldn't bother to wonder if the books were written by a man, woman, or kangaroo.

(quoted in Frankel 1964: 57)

Travers believed that using a pen name, as had past female authors, sub-verted chauvinistic dismissal as '"one more silly woman writing silly books" [...] "It's never respected as literature, it's never given a high place in that sense"' (1965 interview quoted in Lawson 2013: 162).

Travers' embrace of her liberated passions extended to romantic partners and domesticity. According to biographical accounts, from all indications Travers became enamored of and entered into romantic relationships with male and female companions. Eschewing conventional domesticity, by the time *Mary Poppins* was published Travers had lived with a female partner for seven years and would soon engage in an intimate relationship with another woman. In 1939, Travers became a single mother, adopting a son named Camillus. Thereafter, however, conforming in appearance to conventions of patriarchal culture, she wore a wedding ring and asked to be addressed as 'Mrs. Travers.' Although drawn to child-rearing, by various accounts (espe-cially that of her son, Camillus), she was not a particularly adept mother. By implication, then, the notion of the perfect female caregiver was in her own experience (as both daughter and parent) a fairy tale.

Currents in the Air

When Travers emigrated to England in 1924 to establish her writing career on a central international stage, she became caught up in additional contem-porary currents that would inform her fiction and nonfiction. She gravitated toward a literary circle that joined cultural regeneration with 'the revolt against materialism' (Weygandt 1904: 426) and, for some adherents, an in-vogue spiritualism, one that became an important backdrop for the Poppins series and returned to fashion in the 1960s. The Irish Literary Revival was a movement connected to Travers' paternal heritage (embodying, as char-acterized by Staffan Bergsten, Irish culture's 'feeling for legend, myth and poetry, and its high-flying imagination' [1978: 3]) and, on the part of cer-tain leading figures, included alternative spiritualities that magnetized the young immigrant. Forming a deep friendship with George William Russell (who wrote under the Gnostic-inspired pen name A.E.), a mystic, spiritual-ist poet, playwright, and editor of the literary magazine *Irish Statesman*, Travers was 'introduced [...] to the meaning of fairy tales, to myths, the spirit world and Eastern religions,' according to Lawson (2013: 88). In a 1966 Library of Congress talk, Travers recalled, 'I came under the wing of A.E. and got to know [poet W.B.] Yeats and the gifted people in their circle, all of whom cheerfully licked me into shape like a set of mother cats with a kitten' (Travers 1980: 11).

Travers' new shape was not only associated with the 'magical phrase and imaginative power' (Weygandt 1904: 427) of the idealist movement's poetry, for which she had already shown an affinity, and the Revival's 'disdain for bourgeois values' (McDonald 2014: 51); it had much to do with contemporary interest in mysticism and other unorthodox, consciousness-expanding spiritualities and ideologies. Travers became a devotee of Eastern religions (including Hinduism and Zen), mysticism, and astrology as well as an acolyte of a succession of gurus beginning in the 1930s and continuing through the 1960s and beyond. These interests were part of nonmainstream world views that 'reflect[ed] the modernist break with western forms of thinking, art and culture' (Thacker and Webb 2002: 114). From her mid-20s on, Travers remained committed to such unconventional spiritualities that would regain popularity in the 1960s as the younger generation searched for universal peace, unity, and escapist serenity during a turbulent decade.

Pointing to the resemblance between Travers' captivation with Eastern spirituality beginning in the 1920s and that of youths decades later, *Paris Review* interviewers inquired,

> What do you think of the contemporary interest in religion and myth, particularly among young people? Do you sense that in the last few years a large number of people have grown interested in spiritual disciplines—yoga, Zen, meditation, and the like?
>
> (Burness and Griswold 1982: 227)

Travers replied, 'It shows the deep, disturbed undercurrents that there are in man [...] What they're looking for is something that they cannot possess but serve, something higher than themselves' (227–228). The referenced spiritualities surged in the 1960s in the wake of the threat of nuclear war, family struggles, antiestablishment upheaval, and the Vietnam conflict, as the counterculture sought what Paul Oliver characterizes as 'a sense of internal, spiritual harmony' (2014: 132) whose pursuit and adoption were associated with 'the legitimacy of individual freedom' (135). Travers noted, 'I'm all with them in their search because it is my search, too. But I've searched for it all my life' (Burness and Griswold 1982: 228). Albeit in a far less politicized regard, Travers was a self-described 'seeker' (quoted in Baker 1999: 124) from childhood, pursuing what she characterized as 'something totally other, another kind of world, perhaps, another way of being. The word "transcendent" might have fitted my need, could I have understood it' (Travers 1988a: 30). This 'Something Else,' according to Trebbe Johnson, was 'the source of the myths and the truth children live by. [...] [Travers described it variously as] the essential self [...] [and] "a particular process of cognition that ... will take us down to the very deeps of knowing,"' 'the elusive essence' (1999: 136, 135). Travers viewed childhood as a phase of solidarity with the universe and instinctive access to elemental truths less obtainable with maturity. Shaped by the narrative preoccupations of her youth together with the influences of her literary circle in the early twentieth century, Travers perceived an all-encompassing harmony invisible to the mainstream: that of cosmic unity among all beings, forms, and actions from the past through the present, resonating through recurrent patterns and figures of myth, lore, history, fairy tales, and other elements of culture. She infused the *Poppins* series with this magical, elevated vision of transcendent solidarity—paradoxically, perceptible only to its figures of counterculturalism or countercultural sympathies.

Travers' alliances with movements and ideologies that directly challenged the prevailing cultural order continued to grow through the 1930s. In 1933, one year before the publication of *Mary Poppins*, Travers met and formed a close relationship with Alfred Orage, theosophist, literary critic, economic reform advocate, and former editor of *The New Age* (*TNA*), an influential British socialist magazine devoted to modern literature and politics. Peter Jackson observes, Orage's 'journalism [was that of] a political modernist,' one who during World War I 'believed the capitalist system was on the verge of collapse' (Jackson 2012: 38). *TNA* was a magazine in which, Robert Scholes notes, 'spiritualism was part of the culture' and whose contributors 'were always "on the left," but it was a turbulent, volatile left, in which anarchism and authoritarianism rubbed shoulders, and politics mixed with art more deeply than in other places' (Scholes n.d.). In 1933, Orage was editor of *The New English Weekly* (*TNEW*), characterized by *Time* as a new incarnation of his former magazine ('New English Weekly' 1932: 35). Travers became *TNEW*'s drama critic and contributed poetry as well as essays. Continuing to write about spiritualism, legend, and lore for decades, in the 1970s she became consulting editor and a frequent contributor to *Parabola*, a magazine devoted to Eastern spirituality and myth. Travers' amplified cultural interests and concerns invested the Poppins books with defiance of dominant systems, escapism, and visions of cosmic universality, among other orientations that would harmonize with sensibilities of the young in the mid-twentieth century.

Although by her own account Travers did not consciously infuse *Mary Poppins* with the alternative spiritualism to which she had become so committed, others identified such elements from the beginning. A.E. viewed Poppins as a contemporary incarnation of the Hindu mother goddess Kali (Burness and Griswold 1982: 214). Further, Travers recalled, 'My Zen master [...] told me that every one [...] of the Mary Poppins stories is in essence a Zen story' (quoted in 218). Consequently, Travers perceived the title character and her adventures at least in part as modern figurations of Eastern spirituality and feminine power. Travers explained that she had come to see that '[Poppins] is either the Mother Goddess or one of her creatures—that is, if we're going to look for mythological or fairy-tale origins of *Mary Poppins*' (quoted in ibid.). Allying the 'mother goddess' with the feminist movement, which she viewed with a certain skepticism, Travers explained,

> I think women's liberation is, in a way, an aspect of realizing the Divine Mother. Not that I think women's libbers are Divine Mothers. [...] But I think the feminine principle, which we could say the Divine Mother embodies, is rising.
>
> (quoted in 228)[3]

Origin Tale: Poppins' Incarnation

In 1964, Travers explained, 'I think the idea of Mary Poppins has been blowing in and out of me, like a curtain at a window, all my life' (Fox 1996: B14). According to the origin tale, the character was a childhood creation: as a girl, Travers began to weave Poppins fantasies for her sisters (Travers 1988b: G4). A subsequent aura of Poppins has been detected in Travers' 1923 published poem, 'The Nurse's Lullaby': 'Hush, little love, for the feet of Dusk/Stir softly through the air./And Mary the Mother comes to set/A star within your hair [...] And Mary's mouth on your mouth shall fill/The drowsy night with dreams' (quoted in Lawson 2013: 72). On the heels of this ethereal, poetic Mary, who calms the children by transporting an embracing cosmos and dreamy experiences to the nursery, the magical caretaker figure would next materialize as a young woman inhabiting a quotidian world wherein she opens up new vistas.

Travers' signature character entered popular culture in a 1926 short story, 'Mary Poppins and the Match-Man,' published in the *Christchurch Sun*, a New Zealand newspaper. She makes her first appearance as a teenager savoring freedoms apart from and against the backdrop of her position in the family. Poppins is incarnated as a 17-year-old 'underneath nurse' caring for the four Banks children. Temporarily liberated from her responsibility for maintaining the nuclear family, Poppins is introduced outside of the Banks home on her day off. The independent, self-satisfied young woman (accoutred with a parrot-headed umbrella later carried through Travers' books and onto the screen) heads to an outing with match seller and sidewalk chalk artist Bert. Together the pair, whose mutual love is declared by the narrator, embark on a fantastical experience. Led by the struggling artist Bert, who is an amiable social outsider, the 'enchanted girl' enters his chalk drawing of the countryside. Thereupon, they appear in new clothing: Bert sports 'a straw hat and a bright striped coat and white flannel trousers' while Mary wears a hat with a feather and white gloves. In further details that would eventually make their way into the film, the couple enjoy tea served by waiters and ride merry-go-round horses through the countryside before they return from their literally picturesque afternoon by stepping out of the drawing. This adventure, which would become the basis for *Mary Poppins'* second chapter (also without the children's accompaniment) and eventually the 'Jolly Holiday' sequence in the Disney musical, concludes with her return to the Banks residence. Responding to the inquisitive young Jane and Michael, Poppins explains that she has been 'In Faeryland.' She then indoctrinates the youths in liberating realms of individual consciousness. When they venture that she has visited the world of popular fictional characters, she remarks, 'I expect [...] that everyone's got a Faeryland of their own!' In effect, Poppins enlightens the children on their capacities to formulate unbound visions of an ideal order.

The Poppins who proceeds through Travers' book series first arrives in London during the 1930s, a Depression-infused backdrop for the many instabilities of domestic life. Within this more contemporary and somber milieu than Disney's 1910 Edwardian setting, the patriarchal family lives with a handful of servants in an emblematically 'rather dilapidated house' (Travers 1997: 1) sustained by the barely sufficient wages of banker George Banks, a beleaguered functionary of the capitalist system.[4] Beset by domestic problems, George urges his overwhelmed wife to remedy the troubling vacancy created upon their nanny's disappearance by advertising in the newspaper for a replacement—essentially a mass media declaration of the nuclear family's deficiency. The household is set to rights by the materialization of Poppins, who blows in on currents of change, the East Wind. Combining sternness and enchanting fantasy, groundedness and elevation, propriety and subversion of the conventional order, this powerful spirit transports an uplifting unorthodoxy to the young residents of the 'dilapidated house.' Poppins assumes the position with a rebellious haughtiness by which both adults and children are taken aback. Announcing herself as a figure of antiestablishment modernity, one defiantly liberated from domestic life's traditional strictures, during her interview with Mrs. Banks, Poppins 'firmly' states, '"I make it a rule never to give references. [...] A very old-fashioned idea, to *my* mind [...] *Quite* out of date [...]"' (8).

In *Mary Poppins'* 11 episodic chapters—considered by some a modernist defiance of the linear narrative (Thacker and Webb 2002: 117)—the title character brings order to the nursery and in general, as has been suggested, tranquility to the family as a whole (see, for example, Silverman and Silverman 2016: 144). She achieves this effect largely by liberating the children's imaginations and bodies from dominant forces of gravity. Poppins opens portals to a series of mind-boggling outings. Engaging in what Sharon Smulders terms an 'escapist retreat' (2014: 81), as in Travers' 1926 short story, Poppins and Bert enter one of his chalk sidewalk pictures for a magical afternoon tea and countryside ride on merry-go-round horses.[5] In other episodes transliterated into Disney's musical, Poppins, Jane, and Michael visit the literally and figuratively ebullient Uncle Albert, whose mirth buoys him to the ceiling, where they join him when the youths become hooked on his 'laughing gas' high; later, Poppins speaks with truant neighborhood dog Andrew, in 'wild flight' (Travers 1997: 54) from his 'luxurious life' (50) to socialize with a lowborn mutt.

Poppins' practices introduce the children to unorthodox cosmic experiences unadapted to the screen. Her birthday is hallucinogenically celebrated in a zoo where pompous and intolerant adults (including Admiral Boom) as well as greedy children are caged for exhibition to curious, genteel animals; there she is feted by creatures who form a 'Grand Chain' and dance around her in a circle. Thacker and Webb observe,

> It is the freed animals who are noble and gracious. Travers is implying that it is impossible to understand the world from a humanist perspective of tolerance and interrelationship if we are trapped within the cage of materialist reality and cruelty. She is also suggesting, through drawing on Eastern philosophy and mythology [...] that the hierarchical power structures of Western culture and philosophy are inadequate and destructive.
>
> (2002: 120)

Such adventures and others that open the children's eyes to the solidarity of the cosmos span longstanding strict social and cultural (occasionally including racial) boundaries directly and emblematically, manifesting the equality and oneness of all beings.[6] Consequently, the nanny is a figure of multiple defiances. As Smulders notes, the 'freedom in *Mary Poppins* possesses a transgressive quality that undercuts conventions of both class and gender' (2014: 78). Insofar as, under Poppins' guidance, the children are singularly privy to this world whereas they are outsiders to their parents' domain of adulthood, the book foregrounds youth as a province of Otherness and celebrates their unique capacity to savor the liberations of countercultural realms, a sensibility with which the younger generation in the 1960s would be simpatico.

Travers' *Poppins* is invested with increasing Eastern spiritualism as the series progresses through the first three volumes. At times the books directly juxtapose higher mystical dimensions of solidarity with the divisive self-centered preoccupations of the economic order. In the first book, the episode in the zoo ('Full Moon') begins with the children counting their coins—not for charity, as Poppins suggests, but for desired personal acquisitions. The zoo adventure ends with an alternate figure of a monarch in

England, a hamadryad (king cobra), who delivers a youth-centered message of universal cohesion: 'sway[ing] between the children,' the Hamadryad chants, '"Child and serpent, star and stone—all one"' (1997: 175). Smulders notes, 'In response to the capitalist fantasy of private ownership that opens the chapter, Travers thus offers in the reconciling circle of dance a symbol for transcendent unity' (2014: 87). *Poppins'* images of solidarity are also imbued with historically resonant social implications. Bespeaking the context of the first two volumes' authorship in 1930s, *Poppins* evinces a certain Depression-era sensibility regarding the equality and the dignity of the underclasses in all incarnations. Such egalitarianism, combined with an unfavorable view of bureaucracy and banks, aligned with values long embedded in Disney cinema (see Chapter 3) and reemergent in 1960s youth counterculture.

A figure of magical release from the dominant institutional order, the literary Poppins is a character of sharp and compelling ambiguities. She constitutes a model of young female self-determination complicated by her professional domestic role as a nanny. An independent, unattached woman who arrives and departs according to her own judgment (in attunement to cycles of nature, the East and West winds), she nonetheless remains committed to stabilizing the traditional patriarchal family.[7] To accomplish her purpose, she both subverts and upholds the imperialist system. The commanding Poppins liberates her young charges by introducing them to precincts of fantastic experience and illuminating perceptions of nature and the cosmos—loci to which, as maturing children, they are in danger of losing access. Concurrently, she conceals her realms of radical unorthodoxy from the Banks parents who remain devoted to upholding—albeit suffering the failures of—the bourgeois status quo.

Belying her enchanting tendency to introduce the children to wondrous escapist experiences, the novelistic Poppins maintains a chilly, prohibitive demeanor toward the Banks family. The Depression-era nanny is hardened: no longer the gentle, smiling 'underneath nurse' of the 1926 short story but a more mature figure of indeterminate age with an almost unyieldingly stern countenance. Self-assured, as is the *Christchurch Sun*'s Poppins, her novelistic incarnation is arrogant, vain, quick-tempered, and often takes offense. Albeit antiestablishmentarian, she insists on her own authority. Demanding gentility, she does not treat Jane and Michael—nor outwardly view them—with gentleness, though Poppins is tender with the infant twins. The 1934 Poppins frequently snaps at the older children and is capable of 'look[ing] at them […] very severely' (Travers 1997: 65) or 'regard[ing] Michael] with something like disgust' (116). In such respects, Disney's characterization more closely mirrors Poppins' initial incarnation as a gentle teenager.

Travers' Poppins does not suffer the children's questions gladly; one of her most notable characteristics, emphasized by the author and preserved in Disney's musical, is that she 'never explains' (quoted in Burness and Griswold 1982: 225). This principle underlines Poppins' independence—emancipation from the obligation to justify herself or reduce the wonders of the cosmos to formal explanation—and serves as a valuable challenge to the children. Jane and Michael are thus encouraged to develop their own powers of independent thought, judgment, and interpretation within and against the world of their elders. It has been suggested, too, that Poppins' refusal to explain, her resistance to certainty, transmits the cultural perspective of modernism to the youths: Thacker and Webb observe that the children 'have learnt that there is security in *not* knowing, if one has the right philosophical, i.e. Modernist, frame of mind' (2002: 121). Poppins' role as the children's guide to terrains of illuminating unorthodoxy includes encouraging her charges to consider the tensions between the world of alternative freedoms and that of the status quo. Upon their return from magically liberating episodes of free-spiritedness and cosmic solidarity, Poppins consistently denies that the experiences occurred. She thereby indicates that youths' access to dimensions radically beyond the dominant order must remain repressed in the sphere of mainstream domesticity, inadmissible to and unaccepted by parochial adult culture. Nonetheless, it is suggested that this uplifting domain can occasionally be glimpsed even by bureaucrats if they seek to recover the awe of a universe-embracing vision. In rare moments during the series, the otherwise work-oppressed Mr. Banks reconnects with his implied early wonderment at the stars.

A figure of contradictory tensions, the Poppins who can be so quick to snap, so unforgiving and dismissive, guides her charges to new realms of physical and cognitive elevation. Enlightening Jane and Michael, who are approaching their teen years, Travers' Poppins introduces an alternative world free from captivity to the patriarchal system that constitutes a dismal and burdensome not-too-distant future. Expanding the youths' consciousness by contravening the prevailing order, she invests her charges with visions of theretofore hidden possibilities, a galaxy of fantastic, anti-establishment freedoms that include a newly realized solidarity among all forms of earthbound, cosmic, and mythological beings. This world, in which she is a celebrated figure, can only thrive in its invisibility to the Establishment's constant threat in the form of forbidding conventions, codes, and laws. Poppins recovers a universal oneness lost to mainstream adulthood and, without her intercession, bound to entirely slip away from the older children. Such eye-opening adventures—as well as unspoken intimations masked by Poppins' stern exterior—bespeak a deep sensitivity to her charges that endears her to Jane and Michael as a truly inspirational figure, one whose screen adaptation would become even more suited to midcentury audiences.

Within the series' troubled patriarchal order, youth must be cultivated as an age of difference, one of almost complete disconnection from their parents, who are caring but utterly out of touch with a generation uniquely joined with and exhilarated by glimpses of the universe's unbridled possibilities. In Travers' *Poppins*, youth constitutes a stage of life expressly imbued with visions and experiences of emancipating harmony and solidarity, magically liberating unorthodoxy that becomes foreclosed by mainstream adult culture. A starling that visits the nursery explains to the infant twins how the inborn capacity to comprehend all nature quickly wanes with time, lost by the age of one to everyone except Poppins.[8] Poppins' greatest magic is her power to impart the dangers of losing touch with such early faculties of communing with the universe.

When Poppins departs in the original novel, she endows the children with articles of independence. Upon rising from the Banks house, her open umbrella catching the currents of the West Wind and spiriting her away to the upper atmosphere (an exit adopted by Disney), she leaves the observing children with not only an uplifted vision but a compass and portrait. As Poppins earlier demonstrated, the compass, left to Michael, is an apparatus of unlimited freedom, the capacity to proceed in any chosen direction according to his youthful inclination. The portrait of Poppins left to Jane is not just an inspiring memento and token of the youths' new independence from the caretaker, but a feminine mantle insofar as the girl takes on Poppins' position. Tucking Michael into bed, Jane becomes a new female figure of enlightened responsibility, assuming the function of shaping younger members of her generation. Nonetheless, the ending is invested with certain cynicisms. Insofar as Poppins' note to Jane ends with 'Au revoir,' the book indicates that the nanny's return to address ongoing domestic problems—and to satisfy Travers' own Disney-like capitalist artistic motives—endures as a dramatic possibility.

Speaking Volumes

In the two subsequent volumes from which the film was also adapted, *Mary Poppins Comes Back* and *Mary Poppins Opens the Door*, the nuclear family is again engulfed in chaos that anticipates certain midcentury concerns. In the former, Mrs. Banks has abdicated maternal responsibility; in the wake of breakdowns and tensions throughout the household, she banishes the children, complaining, "'I *must* have peace'" (Travers 2014a: 222). The consequently disquieted, untethered offspring seek their own serenity in the park. Michael, chafing against familial conditions and the shackles of mainstream domestic responsibility insofar as he and Jane are charged with caring for their siblings, laments "'I hate this life'" (ibid.). Driven from home by adulthood in crisis and the discontents of childhood, Michael casts upward in elevating entertainment: he flies a kite. His kite connects the children to the universe's natural harmony: 'The taut string running up from Michael's hand seemed to link them all to the cloud, and the earth to the sky' (225).[9] The consequences of bearing the brunt of parental inadequacies and fishing for solace in the realm of something greater are surprisingly uplifting: Mary Poppins is drawn out of the atmosphere.

Once reestablished in the Banks family, Poppins continues to subvert figures of the status quo. She magically cages Mr. Banks' hypercritical boyhood nanny, an elderly woman who denounces Poppins' more liberal childrearing techniques and her character as a 'disrespectful [...] wicked, wilful girl' (Travers 2014a: 264). Poppins introduces the children to other consequences of misguidedly strict rearing and new dimensions of tolerance: the literally upside-down world of her cousin, Mr. Turvy. In a barely veiled reference to struggles of queerness, the melancholic Turvy, a man with a cliché 'limp' handshake who confesses "'I should have been a girl'" (309), associates his condition with wrong-headed parenting. Despite Travers' stereotypical representation of homosexuality and associated paranoia, the book endorses his marginality and the children's exposure to it. Michael is attracted to Turvy's manner of living, remarking, 'I wish I could stay like this all my life' (314), and Jane finds it 'beautifully strange' (315)—both, expressions of modern open-mindedness.

In this book that acquaints the Banks children with alternative cultures residing beneath the scrim of the mainstream, radical enlightenment is highly possible for adults as well. The 'respectable' Miss Tartlett, to whom Turvy has unexpectedly proposed, gushes, 'I have seen the world upside down to-day and I have got a New Point of View' (Travers 2014a: 326). Enthused by her new consciousness of nonconformist lifestyles, she pledges to spread the word: 'It's the loveliest sensation. [...] I shall tell [my relatives] that the only proper way to live is upside down' (320). The consciousness-expanding experiences introduced by Poppins include antiestablishment entertainments that puncture the pretenses of the elite and instate a new social parity, visions that hold enormous appeal for the children and a spirit later infusing the film. The book concludes with Poppins' manifestation as a literal force of nature. The constellations surround her, and she helps produce spring—against the municipal laws that the park keeper attempts to uphold. Shortly thereafter, following the children's ride on a merry-go-round (a detail adopted by the musical), where they become the center of a spinning world, Poppins takes her own turn. The ride gyrates into the sky, and Poppins departs the book as a new star—not only a figure of cosmic unity but an inspiring light to which the children can look. Poppins' final incarnation entrances even Mr. Banks; in rejuvenated childlike wonder, he joins his offspring in captivation with the new star, an uplifting moment manifest in the ethos of the film's final scene.

Written during World War II, the third book from which the film drew material, *Mary Poppins Opens the Door*, is darker in various regards. Beginning on Guy Fawkes Day, commemorating a vanquished 1605 plot to destroy the English political establishment, the atmosphere is foggy and Mr. Banks violently out of sorts. Contrary to the second book's conclusion, he abandons his paternal responsibility—specifically, that of helping the children set off celebratory fireworks. Suffering under the weight of his traditional patriarchal economic role, Banks storms off to work complaining, "'*I'm* only the man who Pays the Bills'" (Travers 2014a: 512, original italics) and brushes aside an amiable chimney sweep. In a line that would become transliterated into the film's most celebrated song, 'Chim Chim Cher-ee,' the tradesman tells Mr. Banks, "'It's lucky, you know, to shake hands with a Sweep'" (ibid.)—a suggestion that the irritated patriarch angrily rejects. With the family in disarray, the genial figure of the underclass exhibits remedial powers adopted by Disney's Bert as one who literally and figuratively alleviates obstructions afflicting the household and becomes the subject of unfriendly fire. Arriving at the Banks home, the sweep is greeted with colonialist bigotry, triggering issues of racism that would resurface in the film. The coal-begrimed sweep is declared a 'Hottentot,' 'Hindoo,' and 'black heathen' by the cook and maid (515). This dark man overcomes domestic prejudice via his own cultural precepts, repeating his adage and conferring its restorative effects on the older children and Mrs. Banks. Undertaking a position that would transfer to Bert in the Disney film, the good-hearted sweep becomes an alternative paternal figure; he escorts the children to the park to set off fireworks. There, Poppins drifts down from the sky, at once disdainfully comparing the smudged children to 'Blackamoors' and 'haughtily' spurning the sweep (523, 524)—prejudicial expressions that would not be transposed to the screen Poppins.

In other respects the literary Poppins of 1943 continues to defy domestic cultural orthodoxies. She serially provides the children access to an alternative cultural, physical, and cosmic order of solidarity and mutual understanding among animate and inanimate beings from land, sea, and air, sometimes directly evoking Eastern philosophy. At last, Poppins again floats back into the sky with her open umbrella. Thereafter, George recuperatively draws the family together, dancing with his wife, singing, and directing their collective gazes upward at a shooting star that disappears—Poppins—leaving the Bankses once more contentedly (albeit, as readers discover in the next volume, temporarily) united in a film musical-like display of joy.

Juvenalia

In the wake of Poppins' popularity as a figure of magical escape from the status quo, Travers made a concerted effort to emancipate the series itself from prevailing cultural biases. Bristling at the literary establishment's restrictive categorization of the books as juvenile fiction, Travers continually challenged mainstream genre delineations, opening up public consciousness to new realms of cultural experience and appreciation.[10] In a 1964 *Saturday Review* interview (as in other interviews and writings), Travers stressed, 'I don't write for children. [...] I don't think *Mary Poppins* is a children's book. [...] there are no such things as children's books. But others think there are. Children's books are looked on as a sideline of literature' (quoted in Frankel 1964: 25, 57). Allying her work—and that of other so-called children's authors—with sophisticated fiction, Travers explained to a *New Yorker* writer in 1962, '"you write for the most perceptive and highbrow grownup—but I find that no place is furnished unless it has children"' ('Mary Poppins' 1962: 44). As noted earlier, in the 1964 interview Travers assailed the genre classification partly from a feminist perspective, arguing that children's books are undervalued because of the presumed female gender of their authors. Elsewhere, she critiqued the genre as a reductive commercialization and academic categorization of literature. In 'On Not Writing for Children,' Travers declares, 'I wonder if [the genre] is a valid one or whether it has not been created less by writers than by publishers and booksellers—and perhaps indeed by people who teach Children's Literature' (Travers 1975: 16).

Nonetheless, a distinct element of Travers' alternativism entailed valorizing youth as set against adulthood. Travers considered a certain order of sophisticated perception to be the unique province of the young, whose cultural contributions included the possibilities of enlightening their elders. Travers perceived the juvenile imagination as one that mined a deep, palpable solidarity with all nature, in effect a form of insightful youth unorthodoxy with which adults must necessarily reconnect for personal restoration. In 'A Radical Innocence,' she asserts that youths possess 'childhood wisdom' that they 'learn very quickly from books and teachers not to respect.' This wisdom, intrinsic to the young imagination, constitutes a liberating birthright according to Travers: 'Every child has it as a natural inheritance, and all the grown-ups can do is to leave him alone with the legacy' (Travers 1965: 1). Travers believed that the transitory early endowment with a unique, unhampered world vision and universal connection remained accessible to adults if they opened themselves up to or maintained a connection to the child within. She explains, 'My parents had, I see now, what W.B. Yeats called "a sort of radical innocence," as though [...] they were linked with their own youth' (ibid.). Travers' George Banks accesses this state of enlightened radical elevation—albeit, by implication only momentarily released from the orthodoxies of adulthood—at the conclusion of the second and third Poppins books, a heightened consciousness adopted, with modifications, by Disney's musical.

Poppins' literary image underwent its own maturation entailing recognition of and challenges to its radicalism. Perceptions of the books' audience and cultural value expanded with the emergence of sociological, educational, and psychological works addressing the problems of marginal, troubled, or otherwise aberrant youths. Whereas Travers' *Poppins*, illustrated by Mary Shepard (daughter of *Winnie-the-Pooh* illustrator E.H. Shepard) remained celebrated as a contribution to the classic genre of children's fantasy, the series became lauded for its capacity to reach recalcitrant young people. *Mary Poppins* is listed in *An Invitation to Read: The Use of the Book in Child Guidance* (1937) as a volume 'recommended by the Mayor's Committee for the Selection of Suitable Books for Children in the Courts,' specifically, juvenile delinquents, whose 'conduct does not conform to that which society expects of them' (O'Brien 1937: 9). Travers' book is categorized among those that

> Appeal […] to the imaginative life of the child, affording him a means of expressing those feelings and urges which his environment denies him and permitting him to obtain release from the less desirable ones [as a] technique in the field of treatment and guidance that has been given relatively little attention.
>
> (10)

This forward-thinking approach is presented as a method of promoting 'socially acceptable conduct' (9). A 1956 volume, *Helping Teenagers Explore Values: A Resource Unit for High School Teachers*, prepared by the Ohio State University Department of Education, suggests *Mary Poppins Opens the Door* (*Helping Teenagers* … 1956: 58). Paradoxically, such publications essentially recommended the Poppins books as avenues to cultural mainstreaming.

Travers' *Poppins* was routinely recognized as a work of modernity as well. In *Reading for Fun*, published by the National Council of Teachers of English in 1937, *Mary Poppins* and *Mary Poppins Comes Back* rank second on the list of 'Favorite Modern Fairy Tales' (Ramsey 1937: 56). A 1949 volume by a New Zealand librarian, *About Books for Children*, describes *Poppins* as fiction 'in which ancient enchantments are proved to have lost none of their efficacy when brought forward in time and mingled with today's realities' (White 1949: 58). A 1958 *New York Times* article on contemporary children's fiction identified Travers and E.B. White as authors of 'modern fantasy' (Buell 1958: 30).

Poppins' status as a contemporary classic encompasses the complexities of Travers' fantasy as that of timeliness, unorthodoxy, heightened awareness of convention, defiance of the dominant order, and adherence to prevailing cultural structures—all of which underpinned the shaping of Disney's musical. A work of modernity endowed with liberating allure, for all its classic attraction the series is invested with certain 'radical' values and other oppositionalisms that not only informed, but were amplified, expanded upon, and also limited, by the screen production. Adapted at a significant historical moment, the film was animated by powerful midcentury crosscurrents which converged with those that first blew Poppins onto the doorstep of 17 Cherry Tree Lane.

Notes

1 Other models for Poppins included, by Travers' implication, a servant who, the author recalled, 'had a parrot-headed umbrella' and 'never *quite* told' the 'always fantastic story of what she had done and seen' (Travers 1980: 8).

2 These included 'The Lost Loves,' published in *The Bulletin* in 1923 (quoted in in Lawson 2013: 71–72).

3 Travers' work contains strong female figures inhabiting what she perceived as the three stages of women's lives: nymph, mother, and crone.

4 The 'Policeman at the cross-roads' in *Mary Poppins'* opening sentence suggests that the patriarchal Establishment stands at a significant juncture during this historical period. Countercultural views of power structures and citizenship are discernible in the suggested oppressions of *Poppins'* Depression-era England, including Mr. Banks' downtrodden condition, as well as in satirical representations of royalty, mockery of government and military officials, and the elevation of marginalized characters.

5 Although their original empowerment has slightly cooled to mutual warmth.

6 Despite the book's general ethos of egalitarianism, it contains racist passages. *Poppins* was criticized and banned from the San Francisco Library for racist portrayals in the chapter 'Bad Tuesday'—particularly, the denigration of Black Americans through what Travers herself would characterize as 'picanniny dialect' (quoted in Burness and Griswold 1982: 220). Travers revised the chapter in the 1960s.

7 As scholars have noted, she is not financially dependent; rather, she blows into the Bankses' lives when the nuclear family is in trouble.

8 Those who have the most natural solidarity with the universe are the youngest, infants Barbara and John, who have the short-lived capacity to literally understand and directly communicate with nature.

9 The Sherman brothers claimed that the kite-flying episode at *Poppins'* conclusion was inspired by their father's love of kite-making when they were children. Yet, such memories may have originally attracted them to the chapter and led to the choice of scenes involving this pastime at the musical's beginning and end. In fact, a detail from the 1935 book's first chapter, 'The Kite,' became

a key transition point in the film. In the chapter, the initially forbidding park keeper soon excitedly reconnects to his childhood through the uplifting activity. His change in attitude is mirrored by the on-screen George Banks' transformed perspective on kite-flying.

10 Various book reviewers commented that *Poppins* appealed to adults as well as youths. For example, the *NYT* critic wrote, 'Miss Travers's children's story, which is also a story for grown-ups' (Chamberlain 1934: 15).

3   Disney's Investment

Mary Poppins was Walt Disney's longstanding fantasy as well. He pursued the elusive nanny for nearly two decades, seeking screen adaptation rights that the contentious Travers at last granted in the early 1960s. By that time, employing his own subversive magic, Disney had already set into motion the process of incarnating Poppins in Technicolor. Perceiving the potential for a blockbuster musical combining live action and animation, Disney oversaw the transformation of the Banks children's pen-and-ink illustrated adventures into a vividly embellished period piece that, amidst its general exuberance, addressed highly resonant sobering concerns.

Imbuing the musical with ritual Disney buoyancy, the production team brightened the setting by rewinding the historical moment to a period predating the Depression, amplifying the emotional volume, refashioning Poppins into a cheerfully spirited, gently compassionate heroine-figure, and punctuating the adventures with elevating songs, among other significant changes. Concurrently, the adaptation accentuated facets of Travers' original vision that harmonized with contemporary concerns including the troubled nuclear family, the oppressive patriarchal culture, social divisions, the imperative to mediate between generations, and the necessity of liberation. Consequently, to perceive the film as a 'sheer frolicsome delight' (Alpert 1964: 22) or 'saccharine, insipid' (Haber 1967: C6), as did the most charmed and harshest critics of the day, was to succumb to the elusiveness of Disney cinema's implications by subscribing to popular orthodoxies—cultivated by the studio's publicity discourse—that overlooked its complex cultural meanings. The widely circulated image of Disney's wholesome children's entertainment obscured the extent to which the literary *Poppins* had become reconstituted as a timely work that proceeded through multiple registers of rebellious social commentary and advocacy, redefined cultural ideals, and exhibited paradoxical investments as commercial cinema.

The musical produced from Walt Disney's pursuit of *Poppins* unites certain classic elements of his oeuvre with modern preoccupations and

DOI: 10.4324/9780429504600-4

influences that were modifying—and complicating—Disney cinema for new audiences. In essence, Disney's enchantment with the possibilities of Poppins' on-screen arrival spanned cultural sensibilities chartered in his original animated films of the 1920s and midcentury orientations that infused his then-contemporary output, when, lacking both a final contract and patience with Travers, he initiated the musical's preproduction. Assembling a team experienced in creating entertainment for new audiences of preteens and teens in accord with the studio's emphasis in cinema and television during the 1950s and early 1960s, Disney shepherded *Poppins'* transition to a fantasy that spoke to younger baby boomers while appealing to (dually magnetizing and entreating) pillars of domestic culture. For the lofty sum of $6 million,[1] the studio's then-second highest budget for a live-action film, Disney committed considerable resources to an Edwardian-set adaptation of *Poppins* that essentially evinced the ideals, anxieties, and burgeoning tensions of the 1960s. The *Poppins* that alighted in movie theaters worldwide addressed audiences through a fully prismatic lens, its captivating, transportive technologies invoking a spectrum of progressive visions complicated by the economic colonialism of Disney's wizardry.

Disney's Story

According to Disney, it began with a bedtime story. Upon presenting a copy of Travers' book to Robert and Richard Sherman, who would write the musical's songs, he explained that in the early 1940s

> I saw my daughters Diane and Sharon reading this book, and they were chuckling, really enjoying it. Then a few nights later my wife, Lil, was reading something and smiling and laughing. I asked her what was so amusing. She said, '*Mary Poppins* … you ought to read it.' So I did. And I think it's pretty good.
>
> (Sherman and Sherman 1998: 39)

By his own account initially attracted to the story's broad audience appeal within his own household, Disney soon found *Poppins'* cinematic possibilities beguiling.

Disney became so enamored of Poppins that he instructed his brother, studio CEO Roy Disney, to vigorously pursue Travers for screen rights. What followed was an extended and difficult courtship that took place over the course of nearly 20 years without a formal commitment. Letters by the brothers, telephone calls, and wires to Travers were accompanied by occasional transcontinental and transatlantic visits beginning in 1944. Throughout the years of rebuffing these advances, Travers' central concern was Disney's potential disfigurement of the already internationally cele-brated nanny. A 1946 agreement for Walt Disney Productions to acquire screen rights to the property for $10,000 collapsed when the controlling Travers 'insisted on script approval, something Walt Disney was not about to grant anyone,' explains Gabler (2006: 596). Albeit extremely leery of how Disneyfication might subvert her vision, Travers became willing to revisit the possibility of bringing *Poppins* to the screen in the late 1950s, when offered tantalizing financial inducements that promised to elevate her fortunes and guarantee economic stability in her later years. Considerably more drawn to Disney's capitalistic than artistic allure, Travers remained defiantly antiestablishment. In 1959, she not only 'demand[ed] 5 percent of the [film's] profits [...] with a guarantee of $100,000 and an additional £1,000 to do the treatment' but in the course of the negotiations again required the extraordinary power of script approval—a stipulation, according to Gabler, that Disney then would approve 'knowing full well he wouldn't honor it' (596, 597).[2] In 1960, she first 'signed a preliminary agreement [...] [and later] a "service agreement"' (Lawson 2013: 248). Disney was unaccus-tomed to challenges against his long-entrenched authority. Insofar as the studio's literary adaptations largely involved stories by long-deceased or, in the case of fairy tales, unknown authors, he principally enjoyed the freedom to reinterpret source texts however he thought fit. Brian Sibley observes, 'It is an indication of Walt's passion to film *Mary Poppins* that he pursued the rights for so long and agreed to a hitherto unprecedented arrangement of allowing the original author a voice in making the film' (1999: 55). Yet, it is also an indication of Disney's subversiveness. His eventual consent to Travers' radical liberation from the standard contract was cunningly artful insofar as once the agreement was secured he ensured that her vision of exerting authorial control over the Technicolor *Poppins* constituted another Disney illusion.

In the power struggle between Travers and Disney, each variously occupied the roles of creator, protector, and subverter of cultural institu-tions. Amidst this dynamic, Travers' unconventional, rebellious approach to the assertion of cultural authority was not far removed from Poppins'. The author, too, was a figure of female defiance to be reckoned with. In fact, the contentious relationship, which itself became fabled in the biopic *Saving Mr. Banks*, allowed certain feminist lessons from the early 1960s to be drawn 50 years later. Reviewing the 2013 film, Sara Stewart observed,

> Travers is one of the few authors who ever stood up to the Disney jug-gernaut, demanding a level of involvement and approval that most in her position were denied. She did it in an era, and an industry, where

women were few and far between and faced an uphill struggle just to be heard at all.

(Stewart 2013)

Yet, Travers would not prevail. Flown to California ostensibly to consult on the adaptation, Travers was instead subjected to the studio patriarch's wily efforts to win her final approval and thereby fully contain the author and *Poppins* within his dominion. At Disney Studios, Travers met with the *Poppins* creative team for ten days in late March–April 1961 to review a draft of the script and preliminary versions of the songs. Greeting the author on the first day, then departing for a precisely timed 'vacation,' Disney left the production team to contend with Travers' strict notions of how to tailor her 'modern classic' to the screen. Recordings and other accounts of Travers' dialogues with the illusorily receptive Sherman brothers, co-screenplay writer Don DaGradi, and co-producer Bill Dover testify to how clashes of parentage and oppositionalism underlay *Poppins*' adaptation into cinema suited for young audiences in the 1960s. During the meetings, Travers alternately occupied the positions of stern, demanding parent and dissident raging against the Disney machine.[3] She strongly resisted efforts to conform *Poppins* to the orthodoxies of Disneyfication. Despite the contractual stipulations that she shortly thereafter finalized, Travers' recommendations (with very few exceptions) were not ultimately adopted. Although in the course of the following few years Travers' fantasy would continue to be reshaped into a genre film, significant elements of her original vision yet remained.

What Disney Saw

Despite the conflicts between Travers and his production team, Disney's affinity for the book remained unclouded. His attraction to *Poppins* in the 1940s no doubt arose from the concordances between the material and Disney cinema, which was essentially founded on literary adaptations. The original *Poppins*' fairy tale quality, its magical elements and characters, amusing and fantastic episodic adventures, blend of realism and the cartoonish, emphasis on children caught in a predicament and in need of rescue, solidarity between the young and nature evoked in part through anthropomorphism, and appeal to youth audiences while spanning the generation gap were staples of Disney productions beginning in the 1920s, including *Little Red Riding Hood* (1922), *Jack and the Beanstalk* (1922), *Goldie Locks and the Three Bears* (1922), and *Alice's Wonderland* (1923), all directed by Disney. So, too, did Poppins' antiauthoritarian relationship with those invested in maintaining strict cultural order align with Disney motifs of the late 1920s and 1930s, most conspicuously embodied by the irreverent Mickey Mouse.

Disney may also have perceived in *Poppins* certain populist-like elements that corresponded to his early works, for example, the Depression-era setting that features the heroism or restorative power of members of the lower social strata. *Poppins* celebrates the elevated capacities of the common citizen—particularly the underclass, including such marginalized individuals as the match-man, chimney sweep, and bird woman. From the working class emerges a community of commoners with powerful capacities, some magically endowed, who act for the good of the underserved or the neglected, in this case principally the Banks children. Other disadvantaged souls are cared for as well, for example, by Travers' bird woman, who sells breadcrumbs at St. Paul's Cathedral, nourishing both the community of pigeons and the children's charitable sensibilities, an episode that became central to the musical. Disney's casting of Jane Darwell as the bird woman directly references populist values insofar as the actress was best known for her iconic, Oscar-winning performance as Ma Joad in *The Grapes of Wrath* (Ford, 1940), a film about migrant farmworkers struggling through the Depression.

In accordance with *Poppins*' Depression-era concerns, Disney may well have been attracted to Travers' troubling portrait of the banking system. The literary father's status as a banker beleaguered by the institution he works to maintain foregrounds the domestic instabilities imposed by the oppressive and inhumane economies of the patriarchy. This figure's condition harmonized with Disney's own distaste for the banking system. Brode points out, 'Like Capra, Disney despised America's money culture and the mindless conformity it engendered. As [a] collaborator […] recalled, "Walt never had any reverence for bankers"' (2004: 28). Disney's perspective on banking was not only forged by his upbringing in a struggling Midwest family whose patriarch espoused socialist philosophy and owned a Missouri farm that failed.[4] Disney's first production company, Laugh-O-Gram Studios, went bankrupt in 1923, and his subsequent company, Walt Disney Productions, faced frequent economic struggles even when well established. In a 1964 interview, Disney recalled pursuing financing for Disneyland, which opened in 1955:

> it was pretty hard for the banking mind to go with it. I had to go ahead on my own and develop it to a point where that they could begin to comprehend what I had in mind […] [I]t's been true for a lot of things in our history.
> ('Walt Disney's Radio …' 2008)

Although, as will be discussed, the process of adaptation resulted in setting the story back in time to the belle epoque-ism of the 1910s, *Poppins* concurrently became contemporized, underscoring conditions and issues that roiled culture in the 1960s. Classical elements of Disney cinema were synthesized with the studio's new midcentury directions, reconstructing Poppins for an audience of baby boomers. This enterprise was accomplished in part by assembling a production team skilled in crafting entertainment for those who were the subject of current social concern and Disney live action features: preteens and teens.

The Framers

By Disney's choosing, songwriters Robert and Richard Sherman played a highly vocal role in shaping the film. He found that their instincts for transforming the source material into a musical were generally simpatico with his own; upon reading the original book, they selected the same chapters that he had for adaptation.[5] Disney was sold, and in 1960 the brothers, then studio freelancers, were hired to work full-time on *Poppins* and other projects. The Shermans' background was atypical for Disney employees; they had established a career writing pop songs in the 1950s and early 1960s. Disney's reliance on the 32- and 35-year-olds, working together with an older, more experienced production team (studio screenwriters Bill Walsh and Don DaGradi, then in their late 40s), indicated not only his respect for the Shermans' work but perhaps his interest in infusing the production with younger talent and a more youthful point of view.

The Sherman brothers were best known for their buoyant teen songs. Sons of Tin Pan Alley songwriter Al Sherman, who had played piano accompaniments for silent films, the brothers' first major hit was the teen love song 'Tall Paul.'[6] The song was most famously released as a single in 1958 by 15-year-old Mouseketeer Annette Funicello. At the time, Disneyland Records was attempting to 'launch [her] recording career […] The song had to be something for the teenage market' the Shermans recalled (Sherman and Sherman 1998: 131). The brothers proceeded to write 35 more 'funny little teenybopper songs,' as described by Richard Sherman (Parker 2015) for Funicello through the early 1960s, as well as songs recorded by teen idols Fabian and Tab Hunter. The Shermans' biggest pop hit, 'You're Sixteen,' was first recorded in 1960 (by Johnny Burnette) then repopularized in 1973 by former Beatle Ringo Starr. At the studio, the Shermans, who would write songs for 24 Disney films and numerous Disney television programs, were considered a new generation of songwriters: 'When we first came on staff, the established composers and arrangers at Disney referred to us as "the rock-and-roll guys"' (Sherman and Sherman 1998: 26). The Shermans imported their ability to transliterate the troubles of contemporary youth into uplifting, story-amplifying songs that pleased mainstream audiences in their first multiple-number Disney film, *The Parent Trap* (Swift), a 1961 comedy about twin teen daughters reuniting their divorced parents. The signature song, a lyrically and rhythmically soft-pedaled rock tune performed by the twins (one strumming a guitar) for their parents, is titled, 'Let's Get Together.'[7] The song's simple lines carry a considerable euphemistic charge, coupling romantic, legal, and erotic implications with broader desires for domestic and social solidarity at the outset of a decade troubled by multiple forms of cultural fracture. Not only is the sanitized music meant to bridge the generation gap by appealing to teens and their elders, but 'Let's Get Together' is an activist song staged to mobilize family unity.

In conceiving the soundtrack for *Poppins*, the Shermans both wittingly and unwittingly amplified elements of the book that resonated with yet other cultural concerns of the new decade. In accord with the shift in youth music from pop love songs of the 1950s to tunes of social awareness, change, and free-spiritedness in the 1960s, the Shermans' music for *Poppins* included the feminist anthem 'Sister Suffragette,' the socially conscious ballad 'Feed the Birds,' and the pharmaceutically prescriptive 'Spoonful of Sugar.' With regard to 'Spoonful,' the possibilities of modern drugs influenced the Shermans insofar as the image derived from the new polio vaccine delivered to youths in the early 1960s via dose-soaked sugar cubes (hence the lyric, 'A spoonful of sugar helps the medicine go down')—in essence, a drug administered to sugarcoat a painful experience and vanquish a scourge of childhood.[8] Consequently, the production number resonates with other then-current uses of pharmaceuticals to alleviate youths' struggles insofar as the lyrical prescription is accompanied by the Banks children's hallucinogenic experience. The scene of toys and clothing wildly soaring through the nursery as a means of contending with traditional mandates of regimentation constitutes the youths' introduction to the mind-bending freedoms of trippiness. Fittingly, couching lyrics advocating a reformed order in popular and established Edwardian-period melodies, including English music hall songs and marches, the Shermans' numbers in essence play out tensions between expounding new cultural visions and adhering to entrenched imperatives of producing mainstream commercial entertainment.

Trippy experiences are, of course, not uncommon in classic youth literature and Disney cinema. Yet, as opposed to Disney's many adaptations of literary works containing magical episodes within the context of the everyday—such as the animated *Pinocchio* (Sharpsteen et al., 1940), *Alice in Wonderland* (Geronimi et al., 1951), which, in accord with the book, contains images suggestive of drug culture, or *Peter Pan* (Luske et al., 1953)—*Mary Poppins* is almost entirely live-action. Via graphics alone, Disney's animated films create a distance between the audience's experience of reality and the hallucinogenic, a fissure that *Poppins* largely closes not only through the palpability of 'living' characters situated in an 'actual' setting but by toggling between the restrictive, quotidian lives of the Banks children and mind-bending experiences introduced by the nanny.[9] This authentic and psychologically grounded young figure continually turns the youths on to alternative worlds apart from their tangibly disquieting domestic condition, introducing escapist coping mechanisms and inspiring, consciousness-expanding visions.

Other key members of *Poppins'* production team, albeit older than the Shermans, were practiced in creating works for preteens and teen audiences as well as for children. *Poppins* co-writer and co-producer Bill Walsh had significant experience Disneyfying contemporary youth concerns as producer of the highly popular children's variety show, the *Mickey Mouse Club* (1955–59). In 1958, the program featured a serial about teen life and high school, the sanitized *Annette*, starring Funicello. Walsh had been the producer of another Disney program about young teens as well: *The Adventures of Spin and Marty* (1955, 1956, 1957) and was the producer and/or writer of such teen-populated live-action Disney films of the early 1960s as *The Absent-Minded Professor* (Stevenson, 1961) and *Son of Flubber* (Stevenson, 1963), films that, as Brode points out, engage issues of individualism, bureaucracy, nonconformism, and capitalism (2004: 80–82).

Poppins' director was the Frank Capra-inspired Robert Stevenson. Declared by *Variety* 'the most commercially successful director in the history of films' (McBride 1977: 1) for his Disney releases (19 from 1957 to 1976), this British filmmaker was no stranger to cinema that both invoked dark issues imbuing ordinary life and grappled with re-containing threats to cultural stability. Stevenson had directed films and television programs in a spectrum of genres, including horror, film noir, anticommunist dramas, adaptations of classic literature, musicals, and comedies. Despite— or, perhaps more accurately, because of—the thoroughgoing somberness of a number of his pre-Disney films, Stevenson identified the director of *It's a Wonderful Life* (Capra, 1946) as a significant influence. Chronicling his interview with Stevenson, Patrick McGilligan registered the connection between the two directors: "'I'm a great admirer of Capra," confided Stevenson, whose own pictures aspire to the dignity and optimism that characterize Frank Capra's cinema. [...] "[Capra's films] say something, and yet they're very warm and entertaining"' (1978: 23). By various accounts not a communicative director on *Poppins'* set, and aligned with the studio's dominant order to the degree that, as Richard Schickel points out, Disney 'liked [directors] who could work efficiently within the house style' (1968: 345), Stevenson was able to systematically produce a Disneyfied vision of disturbing conditions with high cultural stakes.

Midcentury Modernity

The cinema that became, under Stevenson's direction, 'classic Americana' and 'movies a generation grew up with' (McGilligan 1978: 25, 21)—including *Old Yeller* (1957), *The Absent-Minded Professor, Son of Flubber, The Misadventures of Merlin Jones* (1964), *That Darn Cat!* (1965), and *The Love Bug* (1968)—was part of Walt Disney Productions' effort in the late 1950s through the 1960s to produce works that would appeal to a range of baby boomers. As the teenpic was emerging in the mid-1950s, drawing an untapped audience to movie theaters, Disney television and live-action films increasingly featured teens, preteens, and characters in their 20s. The project of addressing the experience of this broader segment of young audiences brought a new contemporaneity to Disney cinema. Albeit sanitized, the studio's releases displayed an attunement to the struggles, unrest, attractions, desires, ideals, and active resistance of older baby boomers and their 20+-aged peers. These films valorized rebelliousness and other forms of counterculturalism; some reconceptualized longstanding elements of Disney cinema noted earlier, such as Mickey Mouse's antiestablishment attitudes. Further, what Stevenson, among others, considered Disney's 'family cinema' (quoted in McGilligan 1978: 25) characterized not only the ideal target audience but the subject matter, often in the form of households that were challenged and even wholly disunified, evincing midcentury concerns.

As will be discussed in Chapter 6 with regard to *Poppins'* reception, rarely has popular criticism of Disney releases recognized a sensibility contrary to cultural conservatism. In opposition to charges of homogenization and conformity, Brode observes that Disney cinema 'embrac[ed] values that are the antithesis of those that [it] supposedly communicated to children' and 'played a major role in transforming mid-1950s white bread toddlers into the rebellious teenage youth of the late sixties' (2004: x). Although Brode makes extremist claims about Disney's role as 'the primary creator of the counterculture' (ibid.), he identifies significant respects in which, from the 1920s through the 1960s (particularly the 1950s–1960s), various Disney films feature young characters opposing the dominant conservative order, address issues central to troubled midcentury youths, and endorse contentious forms of youth expression. For example, Brode points out the anti-capitalist, anti-bureaucratic, and otherwise anti-conformist commentary of *The Absent-Minded Professor, Son of Flubber,* and other 1960s films, the pacifism espoused by Davy Crockett films of the mid-1950s, and the populism of Disney's 1930s cinema (29). With specific regard to youth culture, he identifies such releases as *The Parent Trap*, which not only addresses divorce and the generation gap but resolves them through the unifying power of 'controversial' rock 'n' roll, thereby 'legitimizing [...] youth culture' (14). Other works allied with 1960s youth culture, observes Brode, include the successful 1969 re-release of the originally underperforming *Fantasia* (Armstrong et al., 1940); Walt Disney Productions manifestly capitalized on its qualities as a druglike, hallucinatory experience by advertising the film as 'the ultimate trip' (see also Brode 2004: 17). Brode's very brief discussion of *Poppins* notes its counterculturalism in the form of the hallucinogenic 'Jolly Holiday' and Uncle Albert scenes (26), Mrs. Banks' feminism, Mr. Banks' association with the 'Silent Majority,' and, dubiously, Mary's status as a 'hippie-ish heroine' (93). Yet, the enormously popular *Poppins* constitutes an adaptation that invokes a significantly broader spectrum of contemporary concerns and indoctrinates its baby boomer audience in a range of liberating forms of activism against the Establishment order.

Adaptation: Flipping the Script

Although the screen *Poppins* retains key facets of the original that suited Travers' fantasy to 1960s Disney cinema, in numerous respects the fantasy was recrafted into a genre film more particularly befitting baby boomers. One of the most significant alterations—to which Travers did not object— was that of transforming the historical context from bleak, Depression-era England to the seeming belle epoque-ism of the Edwardian era. Casting the backdrop in brighter, Disneyfied hues, the film rewinds Mary's original time, setting *Poppins* in a more buoyant, optimistic period. The Shermans recounted,

> Travers [...] had set the stories in London during the mid-thirties, that drab period when the world was in the midst of a great depression. We thought we could lift the veil of disbelief and add some color by setting the story back to the year 1910, before the world became unglued. [...] London was more story-bookish, and the remoteness of 1910 would add a sense of timelessness.
>
> (Sherman and Sherman 1998: 39)

However, although the global chaos of WWI had yet to ensue, England was then experiencing certain upheavals that were not so remote from those convulsing the U.S. in the 1960s. Whether the production team was aware of it or not, during the late Edwardian period, England was in the throes of its own radical changes as it progressed toward modernity. The period was one of social activism focused on giving more power to the people: budgetary struggles to economically empower the working classes via wealth redistribution, associated political clashes that led to a constitutional crisis, and the rise of mainstream citizens' voices through labor unions, strikes, rioting, and militant suffragettism. Brian Szumsky notes, 'The [Victorian] "era" is depicted at its historic denouement when the patriarchal powers are feeling the growing pressure of social change' (2000: 99). Among the timeliest of the crusades dramatized on screen, Travers' detached, sometimes gentle but often overwhelmed and exasperated mother, the apolitical Mrs. Banks, was transformed into a strident suffragette, one of the author's numerous dissatisfactions with the film (e.g., see Sibley 1999: 53). One year after the publication of *The Feminine Mystique*, and during the nascent second wave feminist activism of the early 1960s, the women's liberation movement became one of the anchoring displays of antiestablishment spirit in the film. As discussed in Chapter 4, given the reductive representation of Mrs. Banks as a figure of harebrained subservience to her husband and the independent Poppins' association with domesticity, *Poppins'* investment in feminism is one of its most disputed and complicated facets.

The transformation of the literary George Banks, too, reflects concerns central to 1960s disquietude. The patriarch is recast from a largely dreary minor character—overburdened, quick to agitate, distant yet occasionally capable of loving closeness—to a satirized central figure committed to domestic imperialism inside and outside the home. Banks' screen presence embodies socioeconomic pressures of the Establishment, conformism, gender inequality, the generation gap, and geopolitical overbearance. Disney's Organization Man, a financially stable, problematically cocksure emblem of masculine sovereignty—described by Robert Sherman as one who 'expresses an Edwardian self-confidence as well as its darker counterpart, chauvinistic arrogance' (2013: 384)—exhibits comically strict, antiquated attitudes regarding household order and governmental dominance.[10] Among his failings of a nature particularly worrisome to contemporary audiences is the father's alienation from his family; the Shermans, who originally conceived him as a soldier abroad in the Boer War, understood that instead '"You could make the father *emotionally* absent"' (Richard Sherman, quoted in Flanagan 2005: 45).[11] Altering the literary George and rendering him a central focus, Disney's team in effect reoriented the familial tensions and potential remedies for modern consumption. Caitlin Flanagan observes that the mission of Disney's Poppins is 'to transform Mr. Banks from a prig to a loving mid-century American-style dad' (2005: 41). In this regard, among others, the adaptation chimes with British and American geopolitics in the 1960s. Jon Simons observes that, insofar as British colonies were then becoming liberated from the Empire celebrated by Admiral Boom and Banks, 'The shift from imperial order to familial warmth in *Mary Poppins* was very fitting for Britain in 1964' (2000). At the same moment, the U.S. was entering a phase of significant military escalation entangled with the legacy of colonialism. Travers' apolitical Banks—whose presence frames two of the books from which the film was adapted—can be a gentler soul, occasionally connecting with his offspring through his own childlike enthrallment with the cosmos (a value evidently drawn from the author's own childhood experience), associated with the uplifting vision of Poppins as she ascends into the galaxy. Yet, in accord with the fantasies of youths and Disney cinema in the 1960s, the screen Banks' enlightenment is a direct result of Poppins' dissidence. The filmic father is, it seems, more capable of changing in the wake of encountering the young figure of liberating unorthodoxy, one who inspires the children by her challenges to the status quo.

Richard Sherman's account of the adaptation process referenced how a then-significant cultural anxiety about the state of the nuclear family became a key structuring element of the film. Sherman explained, 'the story had no plot [...] We knew there had to be a reason for Mary Poppins to arrive and leave, so we came up with the idea of a dysfunctional household' (Tims 2013). Although both the literary and screen families are in disarray because of the loss of a nanny, insofar as the parents hold larger roles in the film, Disney's *Poppins* is more fully invested in family solidarity. The Technicolor Banks clan is fractured by physically and emotionally absent parents as well as the father's insistence on martinet-like obedience to patriarchal rule, resulting in the children's rebellion against the dominant order and desire for liberation. By reducing the four literary Banks children to the older Jane and Michael, the film focuses on the stakes of such domestic conditions for preteens (and near-preteens) beginning to experience the unrest and uplifting possibilities of radical opposition that consumed older baby boomers in the 1960s.

The Poppins who descends into Disney's film is a changed woman. The cold and snappish literary nanny is reshaped into a gentle, kindly, and often upbeat figure who sensitively guides the children into new realms of elevated experience and perception. Retaining an air of the original nanny's haughty self-possession and assertiveness, she more pointedly crosses class and gender boundaries as an independent woman. Together with the film's increased scrutiny of the parents, the screen Poppins is brought into much greater focus as a figure of social commentary, a defiant young woman who critiques—and indoctrinates the children in remedially subverting—the Establishment. Leading the children on mind-expanding excursions, Disney's Poppins invests the children with free-spiritedness and radically unbinding cultural views, including a sense of solidarity with all walks and forms of life. Suggested as gurulike by some, although Disney's Poppins, like Travers', never explains herself, the musical nanny does verbally impart alternative world views (e.g., in 'Spoonful' and 'Feed the Birds') that, together with the episodes, exert the power to transform (although not unequivocally) the parents, family, and society. In one of the film's most dramatic scenes, the benefits of this investment literally materialize at the bank. Contrary to the book, wherein George requests that the children meet him at the bank for afternoon tea, a get-together absent from the literary narrative (although the bird woman is spotted along the way[12]), Disney's Poppins not only instigates but reimagines the bank outing as an episode of social consciousness for children and patriarch. In the wake of Poppins' musical guidance, the youths' experience outside and inside the bank becomes an occasion for peaceful protest that ratchets up to antiestablishment activism with far-reaching cultural implications.

Poppins' modern embodiment rested, too, on Disney's choice of actress Julie Andrews for the role. She brought to the character what was commonly perceived as a warm and charming youthful wholesomeness. As dramatized by Andrews in her first feature film role, Travers' plain-looking, stern Poppins became an attractive and welcoming figure of enchantment for the children. Given the screen nanny's defiance of the prevailing order, Andrews' virtuous, inviting image constituted in effect Disney's mainstream selling of the resistance, a milk-complected face of opposition inspiring baby boomers and agreeable to their elders. Andrews' generally wholesome image combined with her powers of captivation transported into Poppins resonances of her best-known recent role as Queen Guenevere in the original Broadway production of *Camelot* (1960), a performance that brought her to Disney's attention. Some detected the transmission of a touch of sexuality in the character, yet another element of Guenevere that altered Poppins' chaste portrayal in Travers' books—a hinted-at additional facet of the character's feminine power.

Together with the wholesome screen Poppins' accessory-filled valise, she carries some of Disney's Cold War baggage. The widespread cultural remediation that the cinematic (vs. literary) Poppins undertakes through the children's enlightenment is met with resonant reactionary suspicions. George's constant distrust of Poppins evokes the anticommunist paranoia of the 1940s and 1950s, including Disney's vocal support of McCarthyism. Stung by a bitter studio strike in 1941, Disney, who had considered his employees as family, viewed unionizers and their sympathizers as instigators of dissent within his own 'house' and throughout the film industry. Subsequently, during the House Un-American Activities Committee's (HUAC) 1947 hearings on communist infiltration of Hollywood, Disney became a friendly witness, testifying against purported communists (including employees) who attempted to establish a labor union in his studio.[13] Although *Poppins* contains no suggestion of communism, the film displays certain HUAC-like anxieties about agents of cultural dissidence and social revolution insofar as the patriarch's suspicions center on a subversive presence in the entertainment business. It is Poppins' job to run the show in the nursery—as well as, with regard to the children, outside of it. Insofar as she captivates them with new experiences and perspectives that contravene the status quo, Poppins is perceived by George as a suspect entertainer, an outsider costumed in domestic habiliments who indoctrinates youth in cultural rebellion. In contrast to Travers' books, wherein the parents voice no distrust of the nanny, the cinematic *Poppins* thereby echoes recently consuming home-based political and social fears. Consequently, the film essentially implies that devoid of Mary's upstanding nature the plot would be a cautionary tale.

In masculine counterpoint to the retailored George Banks, the Disney team expanded and transformed Bert into a figure who facilitates the acculturation of children and patriarch to the possibilities of a transformed society in respects that harmonize with reformist values championed during the new decade. The screen incarnation of this key figure combines Poppins' love interest in Travers' 1926 short story (the poor, well-mannered match seller, Herbert, who escorts Mary through his chalk rendering of the countryside) and the nameless chimney sweeps from the second and third volumes of the book series. Robert Sherman described the screen Bert in terms of free-spirited liberation celebrated by youths in the 1960s, as the film's 'ideal,' embodying 'the theme of the picture: "Everyone should find time to discover the magic that's in ordinary life." […] He had no money. He lived his life day-to-day' (Sherman 2013: 378). This Disney figure's freedom from the Establishment and his introduction as a crowd-drawing, sage social commentator who expresses his views through music correspond to midcentury cultural shifts. As will be discussed in Chapter 4, Bert's initial manifestation as a street singer resembles the performance of new, socially conscious music during the early 1960s. So, too, do Bert's multiple associations with high-ness and Otherness evoke attractions and struggles of the new decade. With regard to the latter, through the blackness of the sweeps, the adaptation re-envisions issues of race, prejudice, and empowerment that surface in the books, particularly as introduced in the 1943 volume. Yet, counterbalancing his inspiring social awareness and alternative lifestyle, Bert is concurrently sympathetic to his traditional patriarchal counterpart, George, and thus a sanitized screen presence. Disney's moderation of Bert's character for mainstream family audiences whitewashes the sweep's status as a figure who represents radically liberating change.

The celebrated and problematized Blackness introduced in *Mary Poppins Opens the Door* involves the title character as well. The literary Poppins conjoins conflicting racial discourses insofar as she bears marks of Otherness associated with the sweep, yet exhibits intolerance. Although upon materializing in the park, Poppins embodies a certain blackness by wearing a black hat, gloves, and shoes, the latter of which 'smelt of Black

Boot polish' (Travers 2014b: 523), she voices racial prejudice. Specifically, she is displeased that the children are 'looking like Blackamoors' (ibid.). Under the circumstances, her comment indicates dread that the Blackness appropriated for and contained by white culture threatens to overcome the white body. As will be discussed in Chapter 5, in the musical's rooftop scene not only is the children's blackness embraced but Disney's Mary pointedly puts on blackness and the film addresses bigotry by placing a racial epithet solely in the mouth of an older white male, Admiral Boom. In this treatment of prejudice, the film pointedly welcomes and lauds 'Black' culture and integration—however, via a racist tradition of representation.

The subjects of *Poppins'* transformative episodes, the children, evolve in their own way from page to screen in respects that evoke the changing times. As Travers' book begins, the Banks children are ensconced in the nursery upstairs. Jane and Michael's childhood (as well as that of their infant siblings, John and Barbara) is a space of traditional entrapment by and marginalization from patriarchal culture. Consequently, they commence as the partitioned Other, curious spectators to the adult world with no place in it, a condition that they passively accept. Throughout the books, they are introduced to an unseen magical world, adjoining yet repressed by the dominant order. Travers' magical realm is paradoxically countercultural: it exists in opposition or counterpoint to the status quo, yet is more all-encompassing insofar as it embraces all facets of culture, including the mythic and cosmic, revealing universal cohesion. The literary children's connection to the world is established through consciousness-expanding episodes, yet, unlike in the film, rarely do they experience these freedoms as more than spectators. Further, despite the print youths' stronger characters and petulant displays of dissatisfaction with their restrictive domestic condition, the Technicolor Banks offspring—albeit sanitized as consistently sweet-natured—are in significant ways more assertive. From the outset, Disney's Jane and Michael demonstrate a tendency toward activism. They take their desires and dissatisfactions into their own hands on multiple occasions, seeking liberation, aiming to ameliorate or challenge the patriarchal world by speaking up in their own attempts at what can be termed participatory democracy, and at times actively rebelling. Like the literary Banks children, they are captivated by the countercultural world—which, according to Disney's interpretation, is part of a less mythic, although equally cohesive, order—yet they are consistently participants rather than audiences to it. This active investment from the outset initiates a film narrative in which the entire family undergoes radical, although certainly not unequivocal, elevating change.

As various critics either directly observe or imply, a principal Disney investment lay in *Poppins'* Americanization, the extent to which Travers' observations of and commentary on the English class system and values could be reconfigured to suit U.S. audiences. Albeit produced not only for U.S. but global distribution, of course, the film evinces a palpably (yet, not altogether intentional) domestic point of view. Donald Levin notes, for example, that the film 'replaces cultural narratives associated with the British Empire as a world power with alternative narratives associated with America' (2007: 116). To fully consider *Poppins* a representation of Disney's vision belies the degree to which, despite his prodigious power, the producer was not capable of wholly authoring his work. Taking audiences on a journey through a turbulent decade that Walt Disney would not survive, the musical contains a multiplicity of struggles. *Poppins* embodies tensions among new radicalisms, issues of liberation, and strains of activism with which Disney cinema had long been simpatico, as well as the imperative to reach across his own pond by appealing to the mainstream. In the process, *Poppins* exhibits its alliance to the decade, including the degree to which its struggles as 1960s cinema could not be resolved even by Disney.

Notes

1 The figure for the budget was obtained from *Poppins*'s Internet Movie Database page, www.imdb.com/title/tt0058331/. In certain articles, the production cost was cited as $5.175 and $5.2 million (Davidson 1964: 67; 'Disney's Live-Action Profits' 1965: 78).
2 Travers submitted a treatment that she composed with a co-writer, but it was not used.
3 For example, Travers contended that the soundtrack should consist of traditional English folk music and songs familiar to those in the Edwardian era (e.g. 'Greensleeves' and 'Ta-ra-ra Boom-de-ay') and advocated for an increase in Mary's and decrease in George's sternness as per the book. *Mary Poppins Special Edition* CD (2004) Walt Disney Records, Disc 2, Track 21, 'The Mary Poppins Story Meetings.'
4 The farm and the town where it was located, Marceline, were beloved by Disney.
5 However, Disney was not enchanted by the brothers' initial concept for the plot (Sherman 2013: 366).
6 The song was co-written with Bob Roberts.
7 The Shermans proudly noted that, in writing 'Let's Get Together,' they conceived the refrain 'Yeah Yeah Yeah' one year before the Beatles used the lyric in 'She Loves You' (Sherman and Sherman 1998: 172).
8 Robert Sherman conceived the metaphor one day in 1962, when his young son Jeffrey returned home from school and described receiving the vaccine via sugar cube. The vaccine was initially administered to American schoolchildren between 1961 and 1963 (2013: 377–378, Corona [2021]).
9 This includes merging live-action and animation in the 'Jolly Holiday' sequence.

10 Whereas Travers' Banks is a minor bank employee, Disney's patriarch is part of the Establishment as a junior bank officer.

11 Robert Sherman explained, 'George Banks would evolve slowly ... with a healthy spoonful of Don DaGradi, Bill Walsh and, of course, Walt's contribution' (Sherman 2013: 365).

12 Upon escorting the older siblings to the bank, the literary Poppins shows no particular sympathy for the bird woman or the creatures that she charitably feeds.

13 The hearings on Hollywood ended in 1958. Walt Disney Productions was eventually unionized by the Screen Cartoonists Guild.

4 *Mary Poppins* Part I

Summoned: Poppins and the Imperatives of Youth

To behold how *Mary Poppins* alighted on screen in a fashion particularly attuned to American culture in the 1960s is ironically to first recognize the integral importance of its British setting, whose distinctive skyline frames the film. The rigidities of Disney's Edwardian England and the resultant acts of resistance addressed U.S. audiences progressively viewing their own society in terms of extremisms. *Poppins* introduces filmgoers to a realm of deeply ingrained social, domestic, and generational divisions that engender turmoil in the nuclear family and diverse forms of activism on the part of the younger characters to achieve liberating cultural change. The Technicolor London of 1910 is a domain of boldly pronounced competing visions that alternately cleave its citizens, precipitate rebellion, and eventually mobilize a certain unification through publicly endorsed reform attainable, it appears, only through magical intervention. However much *Poppins* concludes on a widely presumed celebratory note in which through Disney's alchemy all are ultimately joined in a youth-inspired modern order, the final strains indicate that whichever way the wind blows, true social harmony is only a fleeting fantasy.

The progression of scenes composing the first half of the musical advance in literally rising action punctuated by a ceiling tea party experienced in a state of high giddiness. Beginning as a resonant diagnostic of disquieting times, the initial scenes display the afflictions of an oppressive patriarchal system inducing cultural turbulence and portents of significant change, collectively echoing the condition of baby boomers in the modern decade. Poppins enters the intensely unsettled sphere of domesticity and buoys the troubled youths through emotional, imaginative, and physical release, providing access to multiple registers of liberation. Representing an alternative cultural movement, she constitutes a transcendent young force of not only elevation but escalation. Mobilized by the children's appeal for an uplifting figure of a new order, Poppins introduces an emancipating lightness

DOI: 10.4324/9780429504600-5

of spirit, an ethos of universal solidarity and social consciousness, and a spirit of direct and subtle rebellion. Discussing the studio's midcentury releases, Brode notes, 'Disney films challenged the impressionable audience's acceptance of the status quo […] in the sheep's clothing of soothingly conventional family films' (2004: xxvii). He observes that, contrary to the studio's reputation for producing works invested in molding children into well-behaved conformists, instead 'Disney films taught us to question all authority and, when (if) finding it invalid, to strike out against those who would repress youthful freedoms' (xvi). *Poppins*' first half indeed exhibits an unmitigated oppositional perspective. Yet, it looks ahead to a concluding movement more fraught with conflict insofar as the investment in cultural amelioration is tempered by voices beholden to the commercial obligations of selling a magnetizing vision to mainstream audiences.

Opening Notes

As the film begins, in advance of Poppins' arrival the audience enters a domain both foreign and familiar. From London a series of voices call out, bespeaking a territory rife with resonant tribulations, struggles, and fantasies. Albeit a historical fantasy, the finely tended parks, clean-swept streets, and tidily colonized Victorian homes—an empire on which the sun has literally set insofar as it is evening—bear the urgency of the present. Insistently up-to-the-minute from the opening shot of Big Ben (an introductory image of timeliness couched in traditional English structure), the setting presently sharpens into focus as an imperative moment for youth and domestic culture. Despite rigid social conventions, the children are not passive subjects of this empire; at the start, they assume responsibility for reconstituting their condition through active resistance and advocacy, calling for new direction. In fact, the fantasy of Poppins is not that of a spontaneously appearing figure of magical liberation. She is summoned as an agent of change by the troubled youths. Although the children have temporarily unbound themselves from the nuclear family, they are not the only ones to do so nor are they alone in their antiestablishment activity. Rather, they are central figures in a landscape of countercultural expression resisted by the self-satisfied dominant order.

From the outset, *Poppins* keys on the 'now' through voices of change that bear reverberances of the 1960s. Following an establishing shot of the London skyline that constitutes the backdrop of the credit sequence, the camera 'descends' via a tilt down (and slow zoom effect) to regard an assemblage at the entrance to a park.[1] A cut discloses the attraction: a concert performed by a captivating one-man band. Attired in a newsboy's cap and initially playing a harmonica mounted around his neck, the street singer musically urges the audience to 'gather around' as he serenades them with melodic poems 'suitable for the occasion.' In so doing, the singer, Bert, pauses and appropriately, given his headgear, delivers significant news: 'Wind's in the east, mist comin' in./Like something is brewin', about to begin.' *Poppins'* audience is thus greeted by a performer akin to a contemporary musical artist. The harmonica-playing, cap-sporting singer-poet, who exhorts the public to 'gather round' while he melodically detects changes in the wind, resembles folksinger Bob Dylan [see Figures 4.1 and 4.2]. Dylan established his career in the early 1960s, magnetizing audiences with such social consciousness songs as 'Blowin' in the Wind' (1962) and 'The Times They Are A-Changin'' (1963), the latter of which begins by urging 'Come gather 'round people' —comparable to Bert's 'room here for everyone, gather around.' There is a certain kinship, too, between the subjects of address in Dylan's 'Times' and Bert's opening number. Dylan directs his message to the older generation: 'Come mothers and fathers throughout the land/And don't criticize what you can't understand/Your sons and your daughters are beyond your command.' Similarly, Bert's diegetic listeners, largely middle-aged and elderly, are unsettled by his tidings of changes. In the context of the shifting present, as the Banks children will immediately recognize and all will ultimately agree, with the arrival of Poppins, 'The answer is blowin' in the wind.'

   Bert, the audience's initial tour guide to Disney's London, is a model of possibility as a widely adored free spirit. Unfettered by professional or domestic obligations, he leads an idealized, joyfully liberated life. This

Figures 4.1 and 4.2 Dylanesque and Dylan

figure—a composite of Otherness as a street entertainer, sidewalk chalk artist, chimney sweep, and street vendor—is the first in a series of nonmainstream presences whose voices are foregrounded, celebrated, and prove powerfully influential. The alternative point of view from which patriarchal culture and divergent realms are introduced constitutes a significant form of advocacy. As Donald Levin points out, 'the film inscribes the Others with uniformly positive values' (2007: 118). Conjunctively, the respected Bert ushers in a diegetic world constructed, as Lori Kenschaft notes, to 'systematically eras[e] [...] the consequences of lower-class status' (1999: 234). *Poppins* represents the positions of the marginalized as more elevated than those of adherents to the dominant order. The universal selling of Bert entails the dignification and sanitization of the free spirit as an unfailingly polite, tender, empathetic, and upstanding figure, a bearer of wisdom to young and old, and, at the outset of the nondiegetic sexual revolution, a single male of traditionally ideal, wholesome propriety.

As the film audience's chaperone, Bert introduces certain murky tones by transporting Disney's commercialism into *Poppins*. Much as Bert is joyfully unbound, a value of 1960s counterculture evident from the outset when he stands in stark contrast to the staid, top-hatted men attending his performance, his contemporary social message is in constant danger of becoming drowned out by his capitalistic obligations. As the audience disperses at the entertainment's conclusion, Bert overturns his cap to solicit coins. In this gesture, the drive to communicate a message about the winds of change is eclipsed by the inclination to collect monetary change and thereby keep his enterprise afloat, an act of fidelity to the profit motive. Allegorizing the daunting economics underpinning Disney's cinema, Bert suffers the consequences of delivering a message that disturbs mainstream adult audiences: only two are willing to pay. Brody points to the actor's physical embodiment of divergent approaches to capitalism in *Poppins* insofar as Dick Van Dyke, who later appears in a second role as elderly bank chairman Mr. Dawes, plays 'polar opposites, common man Bert and the film's representation of a person who has surrendered his soul to the money culture' (2004: 94). Yet, even the seemingly unfettered Bert is not immune to economic motivations; struggles of the prevailing masculine order are inescapable.

Shifting his social commentary to precincts of domesticity, Bert proceeds as a tour guide to Cherry Tree Lane. En route to the troubled Banks home, he acquaints the audience with a bastion of the Establishment's most far-reaching authoritarian tendencies: the residence of Admiral Boom. This battleship-like edifice occupied by a former officer of His Majesty's Navy, emblem of 'the past glory' (Szumsky 2000: 103) of British imperialism, is dedicated to maintaining the Empire's order.[2] As the first mate prepares to fire a rooftop cannon precisely on the hour, the incendiary nature of lockstep adherence to the dominant system and its impact on the present moment is indicated by Boom's identification of the operation. The uniformed admiral booms, 'Time gun ready?' Levin points out that Boom, as one of numerous members of the British Establishment skewered by *Poppins*, is 'comically dotty' (2007: 117). Moreover, the elderly officer, who clings to militaristic jurisdiction, signals a state of antiquated uniformity that constantly rocks the empire. The literal and figurative reverberations inside British residences underscore the explosiveness of the times. As will soon become apparent in the Banks home when the cannon is fired (causing tilted landscape paintings and other tottering artifacts of British culture), the Establishment's efforts to rigidly preserve the ruling order create domestic chaos.

With the retired admiral's introduction as the first character representing the longstanding power structure, resonant political and military concerns take center stage. The initial subject of what Szumsky describes as 'the film's continuous jabs at the colonial mentality' (2000: 103) not only suggests Britain's antiquated imperialist policy but evokes American anxieties regarding growing military involvement abroad. The 'dotty' hawkishness of the retired Boom satirizes an outdated sensibility whose correlative would increasingly become the focus of unrest on the other side of the Atlantic. Jon Simons notes, 'The imperatives of Empire expounded by Mr. Banks and Admiral Boom became archaic at a time when Britain's last colonies were gaining independence, such as Kenya in December 1963' (2000). Concurrently, colonial legacies combined with Cold War fears were leading the U.S. into the highly controversial Vietnam War, which would eventually claim the lives of tens of thousands of baby boomers. For older *Poppins* audience members, the image of the admiral may have evoked recent highly distressing naval operations viewed in various quarters as incidents of imperialism: the failed 1961 Bay of Pigs invasion of revolutionary Fidel Castro's Cuba, the 1962 Cuban Missile Crisis, the 1964 Gulf of Tonkin incident, and the Gulf of Tonkin Resolution providing President Lyndon Johnson with the power to significantly ramp up the Vietnam War. The latter events occurred just weeks before *Poppins*' 27 August premiere in Los Angeles. By the time that *Poppins* was released, antiwar demonstrations were taking place in major cities throughout the U.S. Insofar as the admiral was fashioned for comedic appeal to audiences of all ages, the cartoonish caricature of the gung-ho, out-of-touch elderly military officer embodies a legibly antimilitaristic message. Specifically critiqued are the martial sensibilities with which the admiral attempts to imbue *Poppins*' youth. Boom later asks Michael, 'Going to fight the Hottentots?' conveying racism coterminous with struggles on the home front and overseas as America's young left for war in Southeast Asia. George will stress, 'The children must be […] taught/That life's a looming battle to be faced and fought.' Boom's serially exploding ordnance imbues the background with the constant menace of military action shaking the foundations of domestic culture.

The camera's entry into the Banks home opens the door to yet different strains of problematized militancy. This domestic space is initially one of female activism by women in the throes of repudiating the prescribed positions in which they have been held captive. As the scene begins, the strong-willed Katie Nanna (Elsa Lanchester), who tends to the children, is in the process of abdicating her role. In effect testifying to the failures of a patriarchal approach to child-rearing, this masculinized figure wearing a tie, button-down collared shirt, and belt declares, 'those little beasts have run away from me for the last time.' An authoritarian reviled not only by the children, whose rebelliousness causes her outrage, Katie Nanna is renounced by the cook (Reta Shaw) for her antisocial 'high and mighty ways.' The characterization is ironically indicative of the antidote to this condition: the resigning caretaker will be replaced by a nanny with magically appealing literal and inspiring 'high and mighty ways,' a radical re-embodiment of these qualities that brings a new, elevated order to the space of domestic turmoil.

Katie Nanna's resignation foregrounds the status of the home as a site of abandonment; the nuclear family is fractured to the degree that all its members have taken flight. Into these troubled circumstances manifesting domestic concerns of the 1960s enters feminist crusader Winifred Banks (Glynis Johns). Inspired by a day of combative public activism, the mistress of the household, wearing a sash emblazoned 'Votes for Women,' enters singing a protest song: 'We're clearly soldiers in petticoats/And dauntless crusaders for women's votes [...] /Political equality and equal rights with men [...] /No more the meek and mild subservients we/We're fighting for our rights, militantly.'[3] As she sings the anthem, Winifred distributes sashes to the female servants and joins arms with them, uniting women of separate classes in lifting their collective feminist voices [see Figure 4.3]. A 1910 suffragette entering Disney's screen at a moment when second-wave feminism of the 1960s was emerging, Winifred marches feminist rhetoric directly into the home for the regard of cinemagoers. Urging women to 'cast off the shackles of yesterday,' she underscores the modern moment as one of imperative female rebellion.

As important as the independent female voice proves to *Poppins*, the representation of Winifred constitutes the most controversial in the film. The disjunction between Winifred's rousing militancy and pronounced submission to her husband has been recognized for its obvious irony—irony perceived as more troubling by some commentators than others. Quick to repudiate feminism and egalitarian sisterhood in anticipation of George's return, upon concluding the anthem Winifred removes her sash and reinstates traditional patriarchal structures, commanding the maid (Hermione Baddeley), 'Ellen,

Figure 4.3 A momentary show of feminist solidarity: Winifred flanked by her
domestics

put these things away. You know how the cause infuriates Mr. Banks.' Further,
throughout the scene she has consistently ignored the voice of another woman
actively unshackling herself from an oppressive domestic role: the resigning
Katie Nanna. In the throes of her advocacies, Winifred remains oblivious to
her children's absence. Scholars and critics have generally treated Winifred's
embodiment of the feminist movement as dismissive. Identifying 'Sister
Suffragette' as a 'liberal feminist anthem,' Chris Cuomo notes, 'Winifred's
activism […] is portrayed as somewhat silly and ineffectual. In fact, it's not
regarded as a serious threat to the family, the children, or the Crown. It can
be ignored' (1995: 214, 215). Ana Stevenson considers Winifred 'a composite
representation that […] implicitly supports women's suffrage while ridiculing
the suffragists themselves' (2018: 70). Given that Winifred appears five and a
half minutes after the opening credits singing 'Sister Suffragette,' the feminist
movement and struggles of advocacy are brought to the fore. In fact, Winifred's
activism suggests how sweeping change can be achieved; eight years after
the film's events, English women won the right to vote. Concurrently, she
introduces the difficulties of translating advocacy to the literal home front.
Winifred suggests that she is fully cognizant of her sacrifice as a largely absentee parent and protestor for the benefit of younger generations. Singing 'Our
daughters' daughters will adore us,' Winifred indicates that she has knowingly
relinquished present maternal devotion for a cause whose full benefits will be
conferred not on young Jane but women of the 1960s.

Yet, by implication, Winifred's radicalism is inspiring in the present as
well. Fashioning the Banks home into a space of modern revolution at the

outset, she paves the way for the entrance of her rebellious children, with whom she continually sympathizes. Further, on the heels of her lyrical characterization of men as 'rather stupid,' Winifred's display of naive submission to George constitutes proof of concept and protest strategy. Her exaggerated deference is perceptible as performance couching an ongoing satire of his bombast. As emphasized by actress Glynis Johns' dramatization, her character turns stereotypical female infantilization and muddle-headedness into a tactic of civil disobedience. When George blusters about the importance of cultural 'tradition, discipline, and rules' as he dictates a newspaper ad for a nanny, for example, Winifred gushes with a touch of wryness, '*The Times* will be so pleased.' Winifred's sugar-coated subversion—one of multiple embodiments of Disneyfication—anticipates the more forthright antiestablishment commentary directed at George by Poppins.

Culpability for the fractured nuclear family and youth discontent is literally laid at the doorstep of both parents with the return of the absentee father. If dedication to radical feminism can result in the abdication of maternal responsibilities that produces wayward children, such is even more the case, conversely, for myopic paternal devotion to the traditional patriarchal order. Whereas Winifred advocates for necessary cultural change, George (David Tomlinson) is unaware of any domestic crisis whatsoever. Introduced as a self-satisfied martinet corseted in a three-piece suit and standard business hours, the banker celebrates the economic stability of the British pound, the grandeur of the Empire's imperialism as it extends to his 'lordly' reign over his familial domain, and the comforting conformism of the status quo. In his introductory musical number, upon striding through the front door, George reinstates the rhetoric, if not the regulation, of the dominant power structure, trumpeting:

It's grand to be an Englishman in 1910
King Edward's on the throne it's the age of men
I'm the lord of my castle the sovereign, the liege
I treat my subjects, servants, children, wife with a firm but gentle hand,
    noblesse oblige

Levin points out that with regard to the patriarchy, economics, imperialism, and the family, George 'shows how all of these institutions are interrelated' (2007: 116). Associatively, throughout the film, as Levin notes, 'every representation of British imperial pretension is parodied and undermined' (117)—a critique that centers on the father. Given the state of the Banks family, George's appearance constitutes the return of the emblem less of sovereign masculine order (he lyrically characterizes his children as 'heirs to my dominion') than of disorder. Cuomo aptly observes that he is the 'failed patriarch' of a 'British family [...] on the verge of collapse' (1995: 214). George's disciple-like commitment to the Establishment is not only carica- turized but his strict conformism exposed as outmoded. Consequently, he transports into *Poppins* a familiar anachronistic figure of the ills troubling youths during the 1960s. The buttoned-up father is in effect a caricature of the Organization Man.

As the physically and emotionally absent scion trumpets his lordly posi- tion in obliviousness to the nuclear family's maladies, Winifred interjects the focus of the film: 'Dear, it's about the children.' The 'heirs to [George's] dominion' have abandoned the home, and the Empire's traditional clockwork regulation has broken down. In the latter's place, a series of cultural ailments crystallized by George's entrance—including the imperial tyranny of capi- talism, the dysfunctional family, the generation gap, patriarchal repudiation of the voices of the young among others, and juvenile unrest—are pressing afflictions of the moment. An indication of the condition's modernity lies in the insistence of *Poppins*' lexicon. George first attempts to reinstate tradi- tional domestic order by placing an advertisement for help, significantly, in *The Times*. Yet, in essence confessing that he is out of touch, he literally has difficulty connecting. When George tries to telephone, he admits his inca- pability to the operator: 'Give me *The Times*, please. No, I do not know the number.' The imperatives of the present are signaled lexically throughout the film; the words 'time' or 'times' are spoken on a total of 106 occasions.

Poppins criticism tends to neglect the Banks children nearly as much as their parents do. Nonetheless, whether or not they are present on screen, the youths are consistently central to the drama. Increasingly true of the decade during which baby boomers viewed *Poppins*, in reaction to prevailing cul- tural conditions the youths have resorted to rebellion. In a resonant intro- duction, the alienated Jane (Karen Dotrice) and Michael (Matthew Garber) have sought peace of mind through escapism in the park. Flying a kite that proved so powerful amid the present currents that they became lost, the youths pursued a form of highness that led them astray. Viewed through the lens of 1960s youth culture, incorporating adult concerns about drug use and wayward offspring, the trip has multiple repercussions. In this youth fantasy, the incident is so symptomatic of the patriarchy's failings that even the police officer who brings the children home advocates on their behalf. In *Poppins*' radical approach to domestic troubles, the officer not only jus- tifies their behavior but endorses Michael's suggestion that George 'help' the children construct an adequate kite. The father is thereby beseeched to reconstruct the family dynamic according to the terms of youth—a form of giddy elevation eventually embraced by the parents and the culture at large.

The youths soon become more directly outspoken. Carrying out an act of civil disobedience following their marginalization by the patriarchy

Figure 4.4 George reacts to the children's manifesto

(George sends the children up to the nursery, then dictates an ad for a new nanny), Jane and Michael return downstairs to deliver in effect a manifesto. In opposition to George's stentorian musical decree that martial law must be reestablished—'A British nanny must be a general/The future empire lies within her hands [...] Tradition, discipline and rules must be the tools'—the children present their blueprint for a pacifistic order. Through the modern activism of a gentle song,[4] the children advocate for domestic reform effectuated by an optimistic, forward-thinking figure who addresses the ills of the young generation with a consciousness-expanding, egalitarian humanism: one with a 'cheery disposition,' who is 'kind,' 'witty,' 'sweet,' 'sing[s] songs,' 'play[s] games, all sorts,' and 'won't [...] dominate us.' In a display of young feminine power that directly confronts the patriarchy, the declaration is primarily written and solely delivered by the boomer-aged Jane [see Figure 4.4]. This manifesto of youth culture, a utopian ideal of peace, beauty ('fairly pretty'), equality, and inspiration, brings Poppins to the troubled household. In other words, Poppins does not appear on the Banks' doorstep of her own magical accord, as typically characterized. Rather, she is summoned by youth as an agent of imperative cultural transformation. In fact, she is called directly by the struggle; after George dismisses the youths' voices of opposition, shreds their declaration, and throws the pieces into the fireplace, the visionary fragments of paper elevate through the ether to Poppins.

Into the resonant turmoil of 17 Cherry Tree Lane descends the transformative Mary Poppins, a magically powerful figure from on high who arrives to inspire the children with an elevating counterculturalism.

Her bearing as a forceful, independent young woman, one who (unlike Mrs. Banks) does not shrink from confrontation with the father, is underscored from the outset, as is the object of her cause. Marching through the front door with her own antiestablishment militancy, she reconstitutes the domestic order, stressing the central agency of the children while marginalizing the patriarch: 'You are the father of Jane and Michael Banks, are you not?' Holding the children's summons, Poppins directly rebels against the masculine system by critiquing its outdated operations. Delivering a line from Travers' book nearly verbatim to the father, significantly, rather than the mother (who is absent), Poppins replies to George's request for recommendations, 'I make it a point never to give references. A very old-fashioned idea to my mind.' She thereby underscores her modern liberation from the status quo and George's servitude to an outmoded past. Poppins proceeds to silence the patriarch by responding directly to the children's description of their ideal contemporary guiding spirit, much to the puzzlement of George, who cannot fathom how his attempt to repress the youths' voices has failed. Additionally disorienting George, who speechlessly accedes to the young newcomer, Poppins places his dominant system on probation: 'I believe a trial period would be wise. I'll give you one week.' Richard Schickel wrote in 1968 that Poppins 'had, in the film, a spunky independence to which any child could respond, and she remained acceptably nonconformist in her ways and views and therefore a useful model for children to contemplate' (356). In her first scene, she demonstrates not only this quality. Sporting the conventional ensemble of a perfectly tailored button-down coat, proper grammar, and a chilly attitude, Poppins enters and thereafter continues to operate as one who, as Szumsky observes with regard to her costuming and physical accoutrements, 'wearing the guise of her society [...] work[s] for change and subvert[s] cultural biases from the inside' (2000: 105). Beginning with this initial encounter, she continually appropriates the presumptive rhetoric of the old guard for the cause of freeing youth—and, in turn, the entire family—from the corsetry of the Establishment.

At the same time, Poppins models not only gender parity but a new, independent female power. Cuomo observes,

> Disney's Mary Poppins exemplifies a kind of feminist hero who lives out ideals of women's equality by being completely assertive and autonomous [...] She is not a stereotypically nurturant caregiver, and she attends to the needs of the Banks children without becoming a sacrificial, self-deprecating mother. [...] [Also,] her affiliations are not constrained by class or even species distinctions. One could say that

she embodies certain liberal feminist egalitarian values and even some radical feminist critiques of femininity.

(1995: 214–215)

Yet, whereas Cuomo asserts that Poppins' activism 'really serv[es]' the patriarch and traditional family, her dedication remains to engendering a more youth-centered, liberated culture not fully obtainable and incompatible with the patriarchal household. Poppins ultimately departs on a note of transitoriness; although George has undergone a measure of transformation and appears momentarily well satisfied, by implication there is much unfinished business.

From the moment that Poppins slides up the banister to the nursery through her outing with the children to visit the levitating Uncle Albert (Ed Wynn) just beyond the film's midpoint, she initiates consistently rising countercultural action. Expanding the children's consciousness from the outset by defying established laws of literal and figurative gravity, Poppins introduces new registers of envisionment, opening a carpetbag of inspiring possibilities for an alternative approach to domestic life. Identified by the would-be inheritor of George's masculine structure, the initially close-minded Michael,[5] as 'tricky,' and conversely recognized by Jane as 'wonderful,' Poppins instantly signals her cultural artfulness; she bears the trappings of conventional domesticity (hat stand, lamp, potted houseplant) in her luggage, to be magically unpacked when necessary to fit the surroundings. Pulling the unwieldly cultural baggage from her modest-sized carryall to suit her purposes, Poppins proceeds to indoctrinate the amazed children in how to exert their own power to put the house in order.

The production number 'A Spoonful of Sugar,' the first featuring Poppins and the children, exhibits the nanny's powers of radical transformation—as well as her obligation to pay lip service to the prevailing order—mobilized to achieve aims vital to youth. In a call to action, Poppins introduces a magically unorthodox strategy that clears the wreckage of the nursery, shutting away the choking overload of miniaturized articles of mainstream culture—all of which the children have toppled. Surveying the room, she begins, 'In every job that must be done/There is an element of fun/You find the fun and snap!/The job's a game.' Upon this prelude, Poppins begins to magically sort out the chaotically scattered shambles of youths' indoctrination in traditional citizenship. In accordance with her elevating will, the diminished objects of patriarchal culture weighing down the space of youth (who have repudiated the playthings, creating a culture in ruins)—the toy soldiers, dollhouse contents, rocking horse, miniature tea set, formal hats—arise and shut themselves away. The project involves empowering the children to purge their space of the Empire's debris. Jane, via a snap of her

Figure 4.5 Jane takes charge of the military

fingers, directs the contents of the dollhouse to return to their domicile and, usurping masculine military command, orders wooden soldiers to march back to their toy chest barracks [see Figure 4.5]. Although Michael has difficulty mastering the method, the young male eventually grasps his capabilities. In the process, Poppins comes into sharper focus; as a figure who reforms the prevailing system by songs and visual magic, she emblematizes the studio's 'spoonful of sugar helps the medicine go down' philosophy. Disney's own 'job that must be done'—in essence, introducing characters and audiences to liberating new realms of awareness and magical capability via imaginative free-thinking that alters the unsettling dominant system—is carried out through the buoyant, sugar-coated enchantments of the studio's signature style.[6]

Magnetized and inspired by Poppins' powers, the children become eager devotees of a new fantastical world view. Led by a figure described by some as 'gurulike' to alternative registers of experience unencumbered by inequities of class, generation, gender, domestic role, and race, the youths are introduced to a radically freeing vision of a magically harmonious, altruistic culture. Peter Kemp observes that Poppins 'issu[es] Zen-like orders for living' (2000: 56), importing an 'instructively magical, mystical and philosophical' (59) approach. Although, much to Travers' chagrin, the film is bereft of Zen mysticism (albeit the importance of living in the present moment is stressed), Disney's Poppins dramatically shifts the children's perspectives such that they recognize a universal oneness and unlimited possibilities. Central to the film's project is the exhibition of how the reconception of culture can inspire the unsettled youths and, in concert, their elders—even if the results, as implied at the conclusion, are impermanent.

Upon the children's first outing with Mary, they encounter Bert, who, free-spiritedly singing, 'I does what I likes and I likes what I do,' has transformed himself into a street artist. Once again, an alternate incarnation of the masculine work ethic, Bert's occupation chalking sidewalk pictures is for all to enjoy—a cultural contribution—modeling a divergent economy of beneficence that carries over into the fictional world of his drawings. As such, his work is elevated; Bert suggestively informs the film audience, 'a screever's an artist of highest degree.' Disneyfying mainstream culture ('a typical English countryside,' punting on the Thames, etc.) through his brightly colored graphic art, Bert again, in concert with the studio's commercial mandate, acknowledges the distasteful yet necessary economics of popular visual entertainment. Both eschewing and endorsing compensation for the successive framed rectangular images lined up edge-to-edge for viewing—reminiscent of a strip of film—Bert overturns his cap as in the first scene and solicits revenue for his work: 'No remuneration do I ask of you/But me cap would be glad of a copper or two.' An independent producer of historically unrespected visual art for the masses, Bert's position echoes the often financially hard-pressed Disney's near-constant struggles to keep his animation-focused studio afloat.

A New Framework

The 'Jolly Holiday' sequence fantasizes an ideal alternative state of existence, one antithetical to the oppressive imperialist confinements of urban domesticity. Leaping with the children and Bert into the drawing of the countryside, Poppins transports the united marginalized group to a wide-open, bucolic space of universal connection among all forms of nature, a habitat infused by enlightened approaches to class, nobility, transaction, gender, tradition, and the possibilities of language. In this liberated domain, the four idyllically reconstruct the nuclear family as one of solidarity, serenity, mutual encouragement, support, and individual freedoms immediately evident when the children uninhibitedly take flight with Poppins' clear approval. Signaling Mary's and Bert's elevated nature, they magically appear in upper class attire, indicating how their all-embracing humanity constitutes a higher order of nobility than that of those occupying loftier social strata. The nanny and sidewalk chalk artist stroll arm-in-arm down a country lane, literally wearing their inner dignity on their sleeves.[7] These exemplary figures freely defy the strictures of literal and figurative gravity; on their stroll, they temporarily levitate above the ground and joyfully commune with nature. Mary and Bert empirically harmonize with all life: anthropomorphized farmyard and woodland animals sing and dance in her presence, celebrating Mary's transformative powers. Barnyard animals croon, 'Mary makes your heart so light/When the day is gray and ordinary/ Mary makes the sun shine bright.' Not only do elements of the experience cohere with the Eastern spirituality that infused Travers' Poppins books, youth culture's growing interest in its tenets during the 1960s, and classic Disney anthropomorphism.[8] The Technicolor excursion constitutes a suggestively trippy episode punctuated by mind-blowing, hallucinatory sights that enthrall the children. At the outset, after lilting 'Have you ever seen/ The grass so green,' Bert rhapsodizes, 'I feel like I could fly' and literally becomes high, levitating above the ground [see Figure 4.6]. Shortly thereafter, Poppins remarks, 'You *are* lightheaded.' The film thereby poses a type of psychic high-ness and hallucinatory experience as an avenue of temporary euphoric liberation from the oppressive, dismal 'gray[ness]' and 'ordinar[iness]' of everyday life.

As the 'Jolly Holiday' progresses, new sublime realms of countercultural-ism are revealed. Reconstituting the economies of the Empire through ideal alternative value systems corresponding with those espoused by Bert, afternoon tea is served gratis.[9] Eschewing capitalism, at the outdoor café a penguin waiter pronounces Poppins' order 'complimentary' in appreciation of what she brings to the table. Shortly thereafter, fully bridging cultural divides between breeds as well as graphic forms in a production number merging live action with animation, Bert and the penguins celebrate Poppins' capacity to transform harshly monochromatic experience

Figure 4.6 Bert gets high

into unbound, intensely multi-hued bliss, uplifting harmony, universal good will, and richness in spirit. Such qualities, fully manifest in the absence of Establishment figures, capture the imagination of and progressively inspire the alienated children.

Modeling the magic of liberation, Poppins guides Jane and Michael toward unharnessing themselves from traditional diversions meant to satiate youth through mechanisms of containment. After some turns on the countryside carousel, Poppins, calling 'Oh, guard,' essentially directs the literal old guard to pull back the levers of power that bind them to the turntable. On her painted horse, Poppins leads the way off the circular apparatus going nowhere for a collective gallop that invests the British landscape with modern antiestablishment values of social consciousness and female agency. Outpacing riders in a traditional fox hunt—as Levin notes, 'an enduring symbol of British aristocratic cruelty' (2007: 117)—Bert saves the literally hounded animal. In thwarting the pursuers (whose attire and identification as 'redcoats' recall British forces dedicated to suppressing rebellion),[10] Bert establishes his status as a rescuer of small, marginalized beings at risk of becoming snuffed out by the traditional order. Subsequently, in a radical display of superior feminine power, Poppins overtakes male jockeys to win a horse race. In an ironic nod to her achievement, in the stands two elderly gentlemen with their eyes closed (seemingly blind to the unconventional results) exchange remarks that in fact signify the importance of this women's movement in the present: 'Excellent time, gentlemen.' 'Perfect day for it, of course.'

The sequence in 'Holiday''s ideal countercultural space concludes with a celebration of female accomplishment. Not only does the crowd cheer as Poppins wins the race, but she is awarded a trophy for outpacing the men. Further, as indicated by the fawning press, her superior performance will be disseminated in the mass media. Yet, Poppins is not content to rest on her laurels. She uses her public platform for pointed cultural commentary. When a gray-haired reporter suggests, 'There probably aren't words to describe your emotions,' she invalidates his traditional masculine assumption that feelings cannot be articulated. Into the scribes' formal English, she introduces the word 'supercalifragilisticexpialidocious,' a countercultural superlative with a significant impact among generations, social strata, and a multitude of circumstances. Bert explains the word's value for the younger generation, singing, 'Because I was afraid to speak when I was just a lad/ Me father gave me nose a tweak and told me I was bad/But then one day I learned a word that saved me achin' nose.' Addressing the song to the Banks children (in fact, the Sherman brothers intended the word as a gift for young audience members to take home from the film) Poppins and Bert present a new, youth-empowering vocabulary that contains the elevating power of linguistic unorthodoxy. According to the song, this mind-bending slang word's metamorphic functions include an expression of complete buoyancy, a way of navigating the shoals of masculinity, and a class leveler.[11] The word that emancipates the signifier from the dominant lexical order will eventually have a liberating effect on the entire family.

In counterpoint to the joyous liberation of the picturesque journey, Poppins reveals her awareness of the trip's illicitness. Back in the Banks home, she represses the children's talk of their thrilling adventure, threatening to 'summon the policeman.' Poppins communicates the importance, even necessity, of cloaking her inspirational counterculturalism in the habiliments of conventional propriety. When the children continue to recall their mind-bending 'Jolly Holiday' experience, Poppins remarks, tongue-in-cheek, 'A respectable person like me in a horse race? How dare you suggest such a thing.' Her comment also signals that it is precisely the decorous nanny's role in indoctrinating the children in consciousness-expanding conditions (including the male-celebrated feminist triumph at the track) that lends the episode respectability. In fact, she concludes the nighttime conversation by placing the highly stimulated children in yet another phantasmal space. Poppins sets them to dreaming through the hypnotic spell of a lullaby; fittingly, her ironic serenade 'Stay Awake' acknowledges their own (bedtime) resistance movement. Via this ritual method of putting the children to sleep, Poppins draws a continuum between youths' traditionally requisite and unsanctioned, nonconformist altered states.

Paradoxically, the trip into a dreamlike, idyllic state of harmony and liberation instills in the children an exhilarating wakefulness that radically transforms the household. By the next morning, following the youths' lead, Winifred, the cook, and the maid are in high spirits and at peace with each other. Further, Mrs. Banks has become a more directly assertive wife. When George complains at the breakfast table, 'Winifred, will you be good enough to explain this unseemly hullabaloo?' she openly resists and points out his inadequacy: 'I don't think there's anything to explain, do you? It's obvious that you're out of sorts this morning.' In a later scene during which her husband sets out to terminate Poppins, the emboldened Winifred speaks up in a certain sisterhood and more progressive understanding of what the powerful young woman has accomplished and is capable of in the future: 'George, are you certain you know what you're doing?' George's disagreeableness at breakfast and his efforts to quell the euphoric mood bespeak the patriarchy's dependence on suppression to preserve the domestic sphere in a state of containment and subjugation necessary to maintain imperial domination. Nonetheless, given *Poppins'* project, George's reaction is a positive sign; the reformation of his orthodox order depends on the patriarch becoming 'out of sorts.'

The second Poppins-led outing introduces the children to a figure of older-generation masculinity 'out of sorts' in the opposite respect. The scene at Uncle Albert's home is a mind-bending vision of an elder male family member in infectiously high spirits. Within the orthodoxy of British culture, this uplifted state (which the senior Mr. Dawes, founder of the bank, will eventually achieve) is marginalized in a shadowy place. To reach Uncle Albert, Poppins leads the children down a dark, vacant narrow street, a setting suggestive of shady experiences. Prefigurations of drug culture increase when Bert, who has opened the door to a dark hallway, concernedly discloses, 'I've never seen him as bad as this.' The soon-revealed problem: Uncle Albert cannot come down from his high. This severe condition is presented as cause for worry with regard to the children. Noting the dangers of Jane's and Michael's proximity to the scene of an uncontrollable high, Bert stresses, 'What about them? It's contagious, you know.' Yet, Poppins leads the children directly in. There, Uncle Albert giddily floats near the ceiling in irrepressibly elevated spirits. Bert soon becomes lit up as well; as he accompanies Uncle Albert in singing 'I Love to Laugh,' he becomes emotionally and physically uplifted, spontaneously joining in the older man's high. When the children become hooked on the irreverent jokes and laughter, Poppins, albeit feigning irritability, allows them to literally become high with Albert. Rising to the occasion as well, she incorporates English custom, elevating a table set with what Bert identifies as a 'proper tea' to the ceiling, whereupon she joins them [see Figure 4.7].[12] Poppins thereby exhibits to the children the appropriation of tradition for the purposes of uplifting countercultural urges. In this state of release, the men's

Figure 4.7 The children, Uncle Albert, Poppins, and Bert (below right side of table with hands covering his head) high together

unorthodox perspective bespeaks an eschewal of solemn daily labors for the spontaneous production of iconoclastic witticisms satirizing systems of manufacture and commerce, among other topics. Bert jokes about conditions in a watch factory (where his brother both fittingly and, according to parodic interpretation, irreverently 'stands about all day and makes faces'), and Uncle Albert lampoons the business of purchasing long underwear. The exchange eventually earning widespread appreciation by George and other Establishment figures proceeds:

Bert: I know a man with a wooden leg named Smith.
Uncle Albert: What's the name of his other leg?

The joke points to the handicap of strictly literal thinking, adherence to the rigid grammar of cultural rules that debilitates humanity.

Much as highness is celebrated, it is counterbalanced by a concern for addiction and the inability to come down, intimating the importance of merging an exhilarating alternative elevation with actuality. That this order of escapism, like the 'Jolly Holiday,' cannot—and indeed should not—last is emphasized by Poppins, who mandates the children's return to mainstream culture, into which they will carry their inspired vision of new domestic possibilities. More specifically, this moment of uplifted spirits experienced in a marginal space concludes with the recognition that escapism alone into giddily high-flown iconoclastic visions creates a vacuum, a social and cultural absence that must be addressed by transporting reformist enlightenment to the space of traditional habitation. According to *Poppins*, the ideal alternative values of the counterculture must be borne by the youths straightaway to the home front, giving rise to a direct and pitched struggle with the patriarchy in which the outcome is by no means assured.

Notes

1 The credit sequence includes a self-reflexive medium long shot of Mary Poppins sitting in a cloud and applying makeup for her dramatic entrance.
2 The admiral, like Bert, detects shifting atmospheric currents. Perceiving an unsettling domestic climate, he shouts down to Bert, 'A word of advice young man: storm signals are out for Number 17. A bit of heavy weather brewing there.'
3 Winifred's modern militant feminism is a clear counterpoint to the antiquated patriarchal militarism of Admiral Boom.
4 In solidarity with the children, Winifred intervenes twice to silence George when he attempts to muzzle their voices.
5 Watching her descent from the sky holding an open umbrella, Michael ventures a kneejerk gender stereotype: 'Perhaps it's a witch.'

 6 Anne McLeer notes a connection to then-modern pediatric doctrine as well: Poppins 'follows the prescription of 1960s child-rearing experts, such as Benjamin Spock, in encouraging self-expression and imaginative play in her charges. She gets them to take medicine through song and games rather than by exerting authority' (2002: 86).

 7 Poppins soon sings to Bert, 'Gentlemen like you are few.'

 8 In the adaptation, like the book, Poppins blows in on the Eastern wind.

 9 The gratis afternoon tea is a detail preserved from the original short story and book.

10 Among their similarities as marginalized figures, the fox speaks with an Irish accent and Bert with an ersatz Cockney one. Van Dyke's accent, much maligned in the press, emphasized his Americanness to many.

11 According to the *Oxford English Dictionary*, the word's use was originally documented in 1931. www-oed-com.flagship.luc.edu/view/Entry/194228?redirectedFrom=supercalifragilisticexpialidocious#eid

12 Brode considers the episode 'The ultimate drug-inspired sequence [...] They engage in yet another mad "tea party," the term hippies would shortly co-opt for smoking marijuana to get high' (2004: 26).

5 *Mary Poppins* Part II
Altered States

Mary Poppins' transformational latter half commences at the film's spiritual apex. As the final movement begins, the youths proceed from the giddy highness of unorthodoxy just experienced at Uncle Albert's to the loftier altitudes of St. Paul's Cathedral, whose image elevates them to the peak of social consciousness. Transported by Poppins' musical oratory, the children re-envision their world as a domain of progressive possibility where, in concert with principles of the common good embodied by the destitute woman beseeching passersby to charitably feed the birds, capitalism's heartless order may be reformed. Consequently, advancing from idealistic visions to activism, disillusioned with the System, the children independently mobilize mass resistance. Ultimately, their rebellion invests the mainstream with certain antiestablishment values and prompts collective harmony—a state of widely celebrated cultural amelioration that nonetheless thinly cloaks disturbing indications of how the voices of youth can become drowned out by institutionalism that threatens to appropriate their alternative principles to reestablish the status quo. So, too, does Disney cinema manifest its commitment to the imperatives of youth as one of problematically divided allegiances between the circulation of an uplifting, imaginative cultural vision and the perpetuation of a mitigating conformist commercial value system meant to sustain its own institution's viability for the literal and figurative ages.

The final transition begins with a scene mirroring George's initial entrance, a second return home from the bank whereupon he attempts to reestablish the dominant patriarchal order. On his arrival, the children, roused by their consciousness-expanding trip to Uncle Albert's, are eager to transmit the experience of their release from physical, social, and verbal laws of gravity. As they greet George, Michael repeats the perspective-altering joke about the wooden-legged man and Jane enthuses that they became high ('we had a lovely tea party on the ceiling!')—together conveying an

DOI: 10.4324/9780429504600-6

exhilarating, changed cultural awareness obtained by perceiving long-established structures from a newly unbound, elevated point of view. However, George cannot fathom their trip nor does he care to do so. Strictly maintaining the gulfs of the generation gap and paternal absenteeism, he rejects the voices of the young stirred by countercultural liberation in the domestic sphere, dismissively declaring, 'Oh, children, please be quiet.' Silencing his offspring's roused speech, George reaffirms not only the dispassion of the patriarch but his authoritarian system's repudiation and suppression of youths' uplifted, alternative visions.

Shortly thereafter, in a compressed rhyming scene that recalls George's first encounter with Poppins, the father reprises his original role as both a figure of the Establishment dedicated to banishing all opposition and a subject of subversion by the artfully defiant young domestic newcomer. In this latter scene, an episode of intended termination rather than employment, George reiterates the dictums of the imperial system that endeavors to govern its many domains, particularly the dependencies of the children. Determined to quash his offspring's exhilarating countercultural experiences by sacking the inspirational figure dedicated to igniting their imaginations, he reprimands Poppins, 'it is high time they learned the seriousness of life!' The father thereby redefines 'high time' as an urgent moment for the youths' sobering indoctrination in the prevailing institutional order rather than spirited liberation from it. Reprising a refrain (slightly altered) from his early song, 'The Perfect Nanny,' George blusters:

> A British bank is run with precision
> A British home requires nothing less
> Tradition, discipline and rules
> Must be the tools
> Without them disorder, chaos, moral disintegration

The culture's straitjacketing conservatism and its accordant paranoiac restrictions as recapitulated by George are parodied as outmoded values of conformism—analogous to the conditions challenged by protest movements growing in the early 1960s. The 1962 *Port Huron Statement* asserts that the 'vast majority' 'fear change itself, since change might smash whatever invisible framework seems to hold back chaos for them now. [...] The dominant institutions are [...] entrenched enough to swiftly dissipate or entirely repel the energies of protest and reform.' The satirized patriarch's lyrics, 'The children must be molded, shaped, and taught/That life's a looming battle to be faced and fought,' in fact express a significant irony; Jane and Michael have indeed absorbed this lesson via the fundamental struggles of the generation gap and their antiestablishment resistance soon to reach its apotheosis at the bank. So, too, does the assertion chime with the 'looming battle' of the Vietnam War that increasingly engaged baby boomers at home and abroad. On domestic soil, battle lines drawn, Poppins will soon undermine George's offensive directly and by inspiring the children to adopt progressive values that lead to outright rebellion.

In the scene, Disney's critique of the older generation's authoritarian order extends to George's symbolic threats against cinema's propagation of youth culture. The satirized George's complaint, that 'popping through pictures/Ha[s] little use, fulfill[s] no basic need,' allegorically impugns the experience of viewing the studio's productions, another form of captivating, consciousness-expanding visions appealing to the younger generation. In response, the title character, whose name is suggested by the homonymic 'popping' that she mobilizes on the part of youths on- and off-screen, animates rebellion. On the occasion of her would-be sacking, Poppins takes control of the cultural conversation, appropriating the patriarch's discourse to in effect undermine the Establishment:

George: They've got to learn the honest truth
        Despite their youth
        They must learn […]
Mary: about the life you lead.

Chiming in, Poppins bespeaks a key project of the film: exposing young audiences to the parochialism of an exhausted power structure. As she, in Simons' words, 'mockingly concurs' (2000) with George, Poppins satirically lists an inventory of bankers' parental fantasies ('[The children] must feel the thrill of totting up a balanced book […]/When gazing at a graph that shows the profits up/Their little cup of joy should overflow'). Consequently, when Poppins pronounces, 'Tomorrow, just as you suggest,' the children will accompany him to the bank, it is implied that she has subversively entrapped the father into not only an unheard-of family outing, but one calculated to expose the institution's deficits. The valuable irony of the forthcoming transport of new values to the literal economies of imperialist culture is presaged by George's blindly apt self-congratulation: '*Capital* idea!'

Poppins' advocacy of the excursion constitutes an acknowledgment that she must leave the true rebellion to the children. As an inspiration, she fires the youths' imaginations with visions of alternative cultural possibilities and guides them toward fulfilling their yearnings for a reformed order through productive activism. By entrusting social action to the young and eventually departing altogether, Poppins in effect acknowledges both her power to impart a liberating new awareness and her inability to abidingly actualize the cause 'on the ground,' for the purpose of bringing widespread radical change to fruition. In fact, the subsequent scene begins with young Jane's enlightened comprehension of the scope of female capabilities in the domestic sphere when, astonished to learn that Poppins has circumvented a sacking and their distant father will take them on an outing, admiringly inquires, 'However did you manage it? […] You must've put the idea in his head somehow.' Poppins' response, 'What an impertinent thing to say!' followed by a comic eye roll, not only acknowledges her powers of subversion but implies that Jane's own 'impertinence' is spot-on, the outspoken female voice of a new generation eager to learn methods of prevailing over the patriarchy.

George's reactionary suspicions, without their darkest implications, are of course not unfounded. When Poppins returns to the nursery, she further redefines George's mandate, merging 'high time' with 'the seriousness of life' through lyrically and melodically elevating music that transmits a new social consciousness to the children. Couching their forthcoming outing to a center of capitalism in softened dissident terms, Poppins explains to Jane and Michael at bedtime, 'sometimes a person we love through no fault of his own can't see past the end of his nose.' She thereupon indicts patriarchy's blindness to humanity, underscoring the degree to which the imperative, as articulated by George, to 'mold the breed' of bourgeois youth entails inculcating a disregard of the needs of individual citizens that lie outside the dominant order's impersonal aims.

Poppins proceeds to sing a melody that constitutes the spiritual high point of the film. 'Feed the Birds,' a poignant lullaby about a highly affecting sight that the youths will encounter en route to the bank, indoctrinates Jane and Michael in the alternative values of compassion, charity, universal affection, harmony, and nurturing the young [see Figures 5.1 and 5.2].[1]

Figures 5.1 and 5.2 Elevated sensibilities: Poppins inspires the children with visions of the snow globe and 'Feed the Birds'

Elevating social consciousness to ecclesiastical tones, Poppins describes an 'old bird woman' who sits on the steps of St. Paul's Cathedral in London each day, entreating passersby to buy her bags of breadcrumbs:

> Come feed the little birds show them you care [...]
> Their young ones are hungry
> Their nests are so bare
> All it takes is tuppence from you.

Set in London's financial district, the cathedral, pictured in uplifting, dream-like soft-focus, constitutes a very different enterprise than the sharp-focus, hard-edged edifice of the bank that the children will encounter the next day. Discussing the song in terms that recall 1960s cultural concerns about youth unrest and alienation stemming from the nuclear family's fragmentation, Richard Sherman explained that the lyrics suggest

> it doesn't take very much to give that extra dimension, to give that extra love. And tuppence signifies little, hardly anything, and feeding the birds means giving to the people that need. And in this particular case, it was the Banks children. They needed their father and mother's attention, their love.
>
> (*Mary Poppins Special Edition* CD; Disc 2, Track 23)

The scene ties such concerns to a reformative populist ethic signaled by Jane Darwell's performance as the elderly impoverished bird woman caring for the hungry creatures that surround her and fly to the upper reaches of the cathedral. Darwell was best known for her powerfully humanized, deeply affecting portrayal of family matriarch Ma Joad in the 1940 screen adaptation of *Grapes of Wrath*, John Steinbeck's Depression-set novel about destitute Oklahoma migrant farmworkers, an underclass marginalized and exploited by the economic system. Accordingly, the forthcoming struggle between the youths and the bank director will amount in part to, as Jon Simons notes, a 'recognition of real needs overlooked by the logic of capital accumulation' (2000). In *Poppins'* reconstituted system of exchange, the more important 'wares' of humanitarianism take precedence over capitalism.

In *The Sixties*, Todd Gitlin observes, 'The counterculture of the young tried to combine two impulses at once: the libertarian and the spiritual' (1993: xviii). So, too, 'Feed the Birds' replaces capitalism with the capital of independently actionable, uplifted social awareness on the part of youth. Poppins inspires the alienated children with a variant spirituality of universal oneness and collective welfare that soon mobilizes their rebellion against the banking system. The snow globe containing the cathedral with birds that Poppins gently swirl to life before the youths' eyes encapsulates the global condition addressed by the song as well as its all-encircling vision—and suggests the ability to shake things up. With the introduction of this object into the nursery, Poppins supplants the miniature emblems of patriarchal society meant to acclimatize the children to the status quo—the toy soldiers, the confining dollhouse—with an aperture to a higher cultural order. As Szumsky notes, 'For Mary, the children become either thoughtless ingesters of their cultural inheritance or critical thinkers' (2000: 105). The moment of eye-opening serenity harmonizes Eastern and Western spirituality, populist sentiments, and other values whose reformations span all divisions in a radically elevated economy of global oneness, a sphere of new possibility within the children's grasp. In a timely paradigm of the inception of movements for social change, Poppins has galvanized the youths through an uplifting vision of reform (nurturing her own small wards through flights of the imagination) that spawns forthcoming activism.

If the social consciousness-imbuing 'Feed the Birds' number, with its multiple cuts to the children's captivated looks, is not enough to underscore the central importance of the young audience's investment in societal conditions, then the point is empirically emphasized in the following sequence, when the two accompany their father to the seat of capitalist order, the bank. Lori Kenschaft observes, 'frequently, we are encouraged to identify with Jane and Michael. We are repeatedly given shots of their faces as they gaze with wonder and delight [...] they, like us, are often spectators' (1999: 237). Although the action is not often technically shot from the children's physical perspective, the bank outing sequence fosters a connection with youth through numerous point-of-view and over-the-shoulder shots in addition to reverse shots of their spectatorial looks, suggesting the position of the baby boomers in the audience. Outside and inside the bank, the children's inspired, highly invested spectatorship constitutes an agitating presence, unsettling to those in literally towering positions who presume themselves to be possessors and stewards of a controlling cultural vision. In the custody of these figures of economic imperialism, the youths turn to active protest.

Outing

The outing begins on a terrain of socioeconomic and moral discord between the bank and the cathedral steps, a juncture that the children enter with heightened social consciousness and the corollary urge to activism. In the company of their father reaching a crossroads amid the spatially opposite sites, the children navigate the tensions between the competing values by resisting George's myopic efforts to lead them directly to the dispassionate bastion of finance. Seeking to pique her father's social sensibilities, Jane points out the bird woman then requests license to feed the pigeons—a gesture that George denies, suppressing both the charitable urge and further mention of his children's countercultural inspiration, Poppins. Immediately, the presumptive heir to the masculine order, Michael, steps forward from the shadow of the bank to assert his investment in philanthropy. Protesting, 'but it's my tuppence,' Michael rebels against the father, literally and figuratively freeing himself from lockstep with the patriarchy as he advances toward the cathedral steps to contribute to the welfare of the less fortunate. However, his act of civil disobedience is stymied as George draws the skeptical boy back toward the bank with promises of a more stirring economic vision.

The children's introduction to the imposing institution of the bank constitutes the film's harshest criticism of the reigning power structure. Upon reaching the destination to which their father insistently leads them, the youths regard an unabashed exhibition—indeed, a musical celebration—of grasping capitalism serving Western conceptions of world supremacy. Jane's and Michael's encounter with the officers of the Fidelity Fiduciary Bank is staged as an assault by three-piece-suited martinets, mouthpieces of the older generation's soulless imperial vision of domestic and global domination. The bankers, invested in the younger generation only insofar as they present the prospect of a cash deposit (hence, indoctrination in an age-old culture of greed), hover over the children as the director, the elder Mr. Dawes, lyrically espouses: 'If you invest your tuppence/Wisely in the bank [...] you'll achieve that sense of conquest/As your affluence expands.' As the pillar of finance creakily proceeds to make his case, his extreme physical and verbal shakiness emblematizes the institution's decrepitude. Chiming in to bolster Dawes' graybearded dogma, George proselytizes to Michael, presumed inheritor of male capitalist rule, that surrender of his tuppence to the bank supports 'Railways through Africa [...] Dams across the Nile [...] Fleets of ocean Greyhounds' (ships). According to this picture of buying into bombastic visions of forfeiting individual worth to faceless, inhuman world 'conquest,' a condition of personal fulfillment—as chorally affirmed by the directors marching in lockstep—lies in fidelity to the Establishment's system of colonialist sovereignty. The bankers' fealty to 'the high financial strata' in opposition to Poppins' preceding elevated message of universal compassion, humanitarianism, and equality is so alarming that the children literally shrink away from the prospect of overpowering vehicles of capitalism transporting imperialist schemes around the world. Such visions of the avaricious machinery of Western economics, built on human exploitation vaunted as 'foreclosures,' 'bankruptcies,' 'debtor sales,' are so unnerving to the younger generation that as the bankers advance on their quarry with such rhetoric, they literally back the children against a wall.

Confronted by the Establishment, Jane and Michael advance from prior inculcation in the alternative values of collective welfare to rebellion against callous, grasping economic imperialism, catalyzing an anti-capitalist movement. This pivotal moment occurs when the shawl-covered Dawes, literalizing the cold-hearted rapaciousness of an antiquated financial order, snatches the tuppence that Michael has repeatedly insisted he wishes to allot to the benevolent act of feeding the birds. This ruthless gesture triggers the youths' revolt against the patriarchal institution's predatory clutches as the children translate their reformational vision into direct resistance. In a physical power struggle, the children grapple with the icon of a timeworn system, prying the coins out of Dawes' hand for investment in a reconceived cultural structure [see Figure 5.3]. Consequently, the youths' raised voices and activism mobilize mass rebellion against the Establishment. Michael's protests, heard by the customers, spark a run on the bank. This outcry against the predatory institution that snatches individual value for merciless enterprise arouses a new public awareness: the economic system is not transactional, it does not support its own patrons ('There's something's wrong. The bank won't give someone their money!'). In other words, the populace's investment in capitalism is not returned. Recalling the bank runs and closures of the Depression, when depositors lost confidence in the security of banks, on screen the tellers' windows and bank doors are shut against patrons rushing to withdraw their savings. The youths' uprising has engendered widespread public uproar that includes the middle-aged and elderly. *Poppins* thereby displays the ideal power of the young, through active protest, to alert older generations to the moral insolvency of the nation's economies. Transforming the citizenry into protestors against a cultural bastion

Figure 5.3 The youths revolt against the bank

that forecloses personal value, Jane and Michael have galvanized the mainstream in a shifting collective consciousness.

The youths' hard-fought liberation from the staid guardians of an outdated order leads them to new, literally heightened realms of social and racial equality. Upon their escape, taking an uncharted route away from the menacing institution of the bank, they eventually encounter the light-hearted free spirit, Bert. On this day a chimney sweep, Bert counterposes the bank's engulfing cadaverousness, the bloodless pallor of the intolerant supremacist system, with a welcoming ebony countenance. Although the subject of criticism as a Caucasian performer in blackface (to be discussed), Bert materializes as the figure of a new, pancultural paternalism, introducing the children to the unfettering, heady elevations and embrace of a subculture that celebrates freedom from dominant domestic structures ('never need a reason, never need a rhyme'). The journey begins when Bert brings the children home, where he acquaints them with *his* own day's work—in essence, clearing out the long-accumulated build-up that obstructs channels of release from the rigid architecture of mainstream life. Piquing the youths' imagination, the sweep introduces Jane and Michael to the converse of the bank's (and the Banks') oppressive structure containing barred tellers' windows, closed vaults, shut doors, and stifling close-mindedness: a wall-less, alternative society of uninhibited movement and uplifting solidarity.

Bert reveals the means of access to liberation from within the edifice of the family, the breathtaking view skyward through the chimney flue, whereupon the magnetized youths, subject to the strong draw of what the sweep terms 'a doorway to a place of enchantment,' are magically uplifted from the fireplace to the rooftop. There, Jane and Michael literally gain a further heightened cultural perspective of their world and its previously unseen vistas. The experience bears certain resonances of a drug-stoked 'trip'; Bert, who earlier informed the children, 'I spends me time in the ashes and smoke,' describes the space where he regularly becomes high as a nether world 'tween pavement and stars' where 'there's hardly no day and hardly no night.' This mind-bending expanse offers new, formerly unimagined possibilities as a space devoid of binary oppositions between the material and the visionary, light and dark, lower and upper classes, and temporal separations. Bert thereby, together with Poppins, introduces the children to a site unburdened by the weight of time and absent of divisions, where—at least temporarily—the elevated vision and its realization merge.

The marvel of a domain in which distinctions between light and dark are effaced includes the suggested erasure of racial difference, a value that the scene works hard, yet problematically, to inculcate in the youths. At the outset, the children's attraction to the space of unlimited elevation imbues them with blackness. Not only are their faces darkened by passage through the chimney, but Michael's face soon becomes altogether blackened by a puff of smoke emitting from a pipe into which he peers and calls out 'hello there!' to the unseen Other. Consequently, the already smudge-faced Bert enlightens the boy: 'It's just good clean soot, Michael.' The designation of blackness as 'good clean[liness]' in one regard bespeaks an expungement of bigotry, sanitizing racial difference for Disney's young audiences. Further, devices of identification resonantly enable the Caucasian youths to experience a touch of blackness as part of their newly expanded consciousness— a form of integration presumably intended to rouse their counterparts in the audience as well via numerous reaction shots of the enchanted Banks children. The main characters traverse the rooftops as a 'Black' family (Poppins, who leads the way, darkens her face even more for the occasion by applying black powder), experiencing the heights of urban freedom and civil disobedience expressed partially in a forthcoming musical number that signals the instant: 'Step in Time.'

The youths progress to a new realm of acquaintance with and appreciation of the 'black' community when a group of soot-faced, black-clothed chimney sweeps literally rise up (from flues) to display their vibrant, non-mainstream culture in an elevating, infectious song and dance routine. The production number presents a rousing call to solidarity among a minority moving in sync as they seize the moment—with some troubling retrograde resonances. Considered by some critics as a ballet, and consequently (akin to the youth-centered musical *West Side Story*) situating the experience of those who Bert earlier declared 'You might think [are] on the bottommost rung' in the realm of high art, the number constitutes a forward, and to-be-discussed reverse, 'Step in Time' in representations of race. The number exhibits a 'black' populace (sometimes in complete shadow) uniting to assert their voices, freed from the enclosures of supremacist culture in a literal uprising [see Figure 5.4]. Celebrating their condition, the refrain 'never need a reason, never need a rhyme' marks an eschewal of the Establishment's dictates by a countercultural movement relishing liberation in a space where, Bert points out, 'There's the whole world at your feet.' In service of additional imperatives, their presentational mode of address to Poppins and the children as well as their motion incorporate bridging. As the sweeps perform cartwheels, backflips, and handstands, leaps, and high steps, physically extending across the gulfs between rooftops and across chimney flues, the choreography thematizes the act of spanning divides.

Albeit expanding the youths' horizons by exposing them to a minority culture, the rooftop scene, as has been noted by Simons (2000), Pollack-Pelzner (2019), and others, is suffused with racist images. The episode steps back in time by reverting to conventions of minstrelsy insofar as the performers, all Caucasian, appear in blackface and present a musical number

Figure 5.4 'Black' chimney sweeps rising up and spanning divides

representing an underclass. Simons observes, 'The Hottentots [an epithet used by Admiral Boom] have been domesticated, allowed a precarious and marginal place in London, though still stereotyped as singing and dancing minstrels' (2000). In regression to more than century-old racist depictions of Black culture, the sweeps (including Bert) perform an impressively athletic song and dance routine with unremittingly upbeat countenances for the pleasure of the audience of the children and Mary, theretofore solely figures of whiteness.[2] Levin observes that the sweeps 'perpetuate a favorite capitalist narrative (the myth of the happy worker)' (2007: 118). Pollack-Pelzner notes the scene's illiberal adherence to studio convention insofar as minstrelsy is a 'mainstay of Disney musicals' (2019: C1). Although an overstatement, bigoted representations including characters in blackface and other prejudicial stereotypes appear in various Disney shorts and features beginning in the studio's earliest decades, including the animated *Dumbo* (Sharpsteen et al., 1941) and *Peter Pan* (1953) as well as the live-action *Song of the South* (Jackson, 1946). In such regards, the film's investment in cultural amelioration is problematized by additional longstanding studio practices.

Despite employing racist performance conventions, the rooftop scene concludes with a disparaging display of militant racism. Reminiscent of the Poppins books' sometimes discriminatory character depictions and criticism of prejudice expressed through epithets aimed at the black-faced sweeps (see discussions in Chapters 2 and 3), the children are not only exposed to, but placed in the center of, the violently explosive racist threat posed by the old guard. Following the youths' hard-fought liberation from the clutches of the Establishment, leading them to new literally elevated realms of social and racial equality at the 'desegregated' heights of the sweeps, the importance of bridging divides and the horrors of what is at stake when this project cannot be accomplished are demonstrated by the incendiary intolerance of another elderly figure of imperial order. Admiral Boom perceives the uncontained activity of an energized dark minority as a Black invasion, shouting, 'We're being attacked by Hottentots! [...] Cheeky devils! [...] Empty the shot lockers! [...] Teach the beggars a lesson.' In the course of what Pollack-Pelzner characterizes as 'a parody of black menace' (2019: X), the fireworks-like munitions discharged from Boom's cannon cause the sweeps to take flight. This oppositional Disneyfication that paradoxically employs racist dramatic practices to eschew bigotry in effect sanitizes the harsh realities of tensions coming to a boil in the 1960s, depicting racial strife while whitewashing its actualities. The condition of 'black' figures stereotyped as barbaric African threats and subjected to the ordnance of prejudice, exhibited as a form of white delusional savagery, is a particularly germane image given the historical moment. In the throes of early-to-mid-decade, violent acts of white supremacy, often by those in blue uniforms (the police), placed the Black community and others involved in the civil rights movement, including increasing numbers of youths, in constant peril. The admiral's rocket bombardment bears resonances, too, of the imperialist and prejudicial military conflict ramping up in Vietnam.

The immediate success of the youths' introduction to 'black' culture is evidenced by their desire to become fully integrated with the minority group, an achievement repeated when the older generation becomes turned on to the movement. Robert Greene observes 'The subversive subtext of the images of blackened, anarchic chimney sweeps rushing through the proper Banks home' (2014). Less a state of anarchy than exhilarating freedom that inspires the entire household to join, the domestic space becomes a locus of unfettered antiestablishment liberation and solidarity among all. When the men descend through the chimney, they fill the interior with an infectious new cultural energy that sweeps up all inhabitants. They dance and sing with the marginalized domestic workers—the cook and maid, who initially protest—as well as the middle class Winifred, whose political activism they support by shouting 'Votes for Women!' Consequently, the domain of mainstream culture becomes a site of harmonized revolutionary social reform.

The revolution is met with true resistance solely by the father. Entering the joyously integrated home, a newly transformed province of social, racial, and gender equality, among other liberations, George only perceives a chaotic invasion of his domestic space. Accordingly, his appearance marks the return of a familiar menace. The 'black' men's lyric 'It's the master, step in time' indicates patriarchy's resistance (including its racist connotations) to modern movements of change, a continually reemergent force of reversion to the 'master's' time. Within this conflict, the inclination of the younger generation becomes evident. The figures of antiestablishment reform represent a radically liberated culture that the male heir to patriarchal imperialism longs to join. The soot-faced Michael is so swept up in the movement that he attempts to free himself from his father's dominion by following the group out the door, adopting the satirical lexicon of the minority as he addresses his father by the moniker 'guv'nor'—only to be detained by George.[3]

In the father's literal reactionaryism, demanding of Poppins, 'What is the meaning of this outrage? Will you be good enough to explain all this?' he admits that he cannot comprehend the antiestablishmentarianism that has inspired and galvanized those within his domain. The stunned and hugely chagrined George comes to recognize that the longstanding order and his place in it have ceased to be guaranteed. The forces of reform unleashed in the wake of his children's rebellion against the bank and the broad domestic appeal of new, uplifting visions have marginalized the 'master' and traditionalism in his own home. Consequently, George becomes doubly displaced. On the heels of the occupiers' departure, he receives a phone call from the bank signaling his repudiation by the Establishment. Identified as the progenitor of youth rebellion against the capitalist system, he is in essence called into the bank as a scapegoat for the failings of his institution.

Disney's Banks Reassessed

Throughout the film, Walt Disney Productions' own overriding commitment to capitalism necessitates submission to the commercial dictates of mainstream appeal via strategies that contain and sanitize the film's antiestablishmentarianism. From the beginning, for example, the musical mitigates Poppins' and Bert's roles as tour guides into countercultural realms via their characterizations as an upright nanny and a thoroughly decent, respectful artist-chimney sweep whose wise amiability bridges all class and generational boundaries. Disney's project incorporates the treatment of George who, albeit the subject of *Poppins'* most thoroughgoing and largely unrelenting satire, is never fully repudiated by the film. In the musical's latter half, the studio's implicit mandate extends to Bert's pronounced empathy and apologism for George's position in patriarchal culture and its inevitable stresses.

Through the mouthpiece of Bert, in multiple regards George's masculine diametric opposite, *Poppins* goes out of its way to express compassion toward the patriarch. The free-spirited, unattached gig worker professes abundant sympathy for the regimented banker—first to the children and then directly to the father, addressing the generations offscreen as well. When the youths, directionless after fleeing the bank, encounter this surrogate protector who leads them home and thereupon introduces them to elevating new cultural visions, Bert precedes the journey by declaring tenderhearted concern for George as well. Promising 'Bert'll take care of you like I was your own father,' he offers all-embracing comfort and harmony, bridging a multitude of divides. Together with creating an ideal, fully supportive, and attentive alternate nuclear 'family,' as a Disney sweep he sanitizes the Banks' present domestic state. Bert explains, 'the one my heart goes out to is your father. There he is in that cold, heartless bank day after day, hemmed in by mounds of cold, heartless money. I don't like to see any living thing caged up. [...] They makes cages in all sizes and shapes, you know. Bank-shaped some of 'em.' Although the soot-faced Bert therein evinces a measure of Uncle Tomism, he dually illuminates George's condition as that of imprisonment in capitalist culture. Yet, his double-edged commentary, simultaneously compassionate and critical, is subversively infused with countercultural values. The 'cold, heartless,' 'Bank-shaped' cage to which George expresses thoroughgoing allegiance is, by implication, a space that incarcerates the entire Banks family.

In the scene following the phone call from the bank informing George of his imminent expulsion from the capitalist order, Bert assumes the role of father confessor. Listening to the patriarch's tribulations while packing away his brushes in the drawing room, the sweep once again sanitizes the older generation's lot while underscoring the fallacies of paternal fidelity to the dominant masculine system. George, conceding the troubles of the cultural structure, dolefully intones:

A man has dreams of walking with giants.
To carve his niche in the edifice of time.
Before the mortar of his zeal
Has a chance to congeal ...
He's brought to wrack and ruin in his prime.

George's declaration of failure is bound up with his apprehension of time as a fixed 'edifice,' the idealized accession to whose pantheon has become foreclosed to 'a man [...] in his prime,' whereas the figures of spirited potential, Poppins, Bert, and the children, negotiate time as fluid and progressive, a locus of infinite changeability that invests culture with ever-new possibilities. According to this liberated consciousness craved by the children, the cultural power of time lies not in the conception of its monolithic nature and the prospect of attaining a permanent standing in the dominant structure, but rather its endlessly transformational prospects. What has been brought to 'wrack and ruin' is the conceit of the prevailing order's perdurability. George's project becomes that of recognizing 'wrack and ruin' as the present condition of mainstream absolutism, necessitating revolutionary reformation of an antiquated culture.

In response to George's projection of culpability onto Poppins for 'chao[tic]' domestic conditions, Bert reframes the diagnosis in alignment with midcentury sociologists, psychologists, social commentators, and others who pinpointed the detrimental impact of the Organization Man and absentee parents on the nuclear family. Once again whitewashing the father's rigidities, Bert endorses George's position while suggesting the fallacies of the reigning patriarchal system:

> Like you say, guv'nor:
> You've got to grind, grind, grind at that grindstone
> Though childhood slips like sand through a sieve
> And all too soon they've up and grown
> And then they've flown
> And it's too late for you to give

Through the hyperbolic trope 'grind, grind, grind at that grindstone' and other observations, Bert reconceives the imperative of parenting. So, too, does this figure committed to liberation, as Simons observes, 'demonstrate that middle class preconceptions may stand in the way of personal happiness' (2000).[4] If George does not appear to immediately comprehend the oppression implied by Bert, clearly the baby boomer-filled audience is not meant to celebrate the father's condition. In softly singing 'It's too late for you to give,' Bert implies the benefits of an alternative economy of parenting, time valuably spent bestowing upon the children vital attention and affection, preventing unrest, discord, and rebellion. Consequently, modelling an inspirational selfless beneficence, the children prove most giving. Jane and Michael, recognizing the impact of their rebellion on the patriarch, descend to the parlor and bestow the tuppence upon George, restoring their father's order to him. Nonetheless, the gesture is laden with countercultural value. The charitable act dually constitutes a repudiation of capitalism as the youths in essence wash their hands of the capitalist system by depositing money back in the hands of the banker. The children thereby dramatize how the System no longer holds value to them, parenting the older generation on the deeper meaning of worth.

When George returns to the bank, the institution is exposed as little more than an abandoned relic. The surrounding streets are vacant and the bastion of capitalism bared as a mausoleum of elderly men. Counterpoising

George's depictions of Poppins as a suspicious character, the film portrays the aged cabal meeting behind closed doors as insidious figures. In a distinct stylistic shift, two expressionistic shots (the first from George's subjective point of view) situate the boardroom conference table at an extreme distance, a looming, dark island of gray- and white-haired bank directors literally and by implication figuratively surrounded by utter blackness [see Figure 5.5]. When George approaches, the chairman's son, Dawes, Junior, a satirized figure of offspring so fearful of rebellion against the patriarch that he is incapable of independent thought, is again reduced to parroting his father. Dawes Jr. equates the Banks children's earlier revolt with the historic rebellion of a young American body politic against imperialist domination, the Boston Tea Party. What follows is a transformational moment. George notifies the conclave, aptly described by Peter Kemp as 'ancient instigators of corporate authority' (2000: 56): 'I shall be only too glad to assume responsibility for my son.' For the first time, the patriarch who himself has followed blindly in his father's footsteps supports his defiant offspring. Then, literally dressed down by Dawes, Junior who officiously rips apart his boutonniere, forces his umbrella inside out, and punches a hole through his bowler hat, George lexically joins the revolt against the System. In a moment of epiphany, newly invested with his children's inspiration, George employs the vernacular of countercultural liberation. He exclaims with suddenly raised spirits, 'supercalifragilisticexpialidocious,' recites the joke that Michael repeated from his high time at Uncle Albert's, and, as modelled by his children, returns the tuppence to the patriarch, Dawes, Senior, thereby divesting himself of the bank. Declaring an antiestablishment revolution,

Figure 5.5 A pointedly expressionistic shot of the bank's boardroom

George banishes the elder Dawes from the new social order, proclaiming, 'It turns out ... when all is said and done, that there's no such thing as you!' In this act of civil disobedience, the now-youthfully uninhibited George embraces Poppins and the freedoms advocated by the younger generation, exiting the bank with a giddy irreverence. In so doing, he endows the institution with the alternative perspective of the children's elevating legacy; the bespectacled, dour bank chairman levitates with laughter, released from the hobbling oppression of his myopic capitalism by the joke about the wooden-legged Smith, another man who embodies a counterfeit pillar of support.

Analyses of *Poppins* typically view the ending as jubilant reconstitution of the mainstream household in uplifted solidarity made possible by a new paternal commitment to the family. Among these, some scholars detect resonances of certain alternative values propounded by sociologists, psychologists, and other specialists during the 1960s. Kenschaft observes 'a utopic conclusion' (1999: 231), one 'which posits the middle-class nuclear family [...] as the site of true personal satisfaction and authentic group loyalty' (241)—a state enabled in part insofar as 'the Banks family has become what might, in therapeutic jargon, be called "child-centered"' (240). Anne McLeer notes that the film 'negotiates[s] the terrain between permissiveness, advocated by childcare experts and conservative fears of declining male-dominance in the home,' posing a solution: 'The father's authority is restored while his authoritarian tendencies are removed' (2002: 88). McLeer asserts, 'Ultimately [...] the outmoded form of capitalism passes away [...] It is replaced by a new order [...] characterized by pleasure seeking, informality, and togetherness' (93). Yet, generally overlooked is the role of youth rebellion and other methods of advocacy in engendering George's enlightenment (e.g. his resistance in the boardroom) as well as the problematized, unreformed cultural condition implied by fidelities underscored and reinvested in the closing moments.

The fracture of the corporate family enables the unification of the nuclear one. Returning home, George invests himself in domestic transformation. Using 'tuppence for paper and strings' necessary to the youthfully uplifting and liberatory experience of kite-flying rather than for bankrolling the Establishment's fettering machinations of imperial domination, he creates for the family 'your own set of wings.' In conjunction, the father displays a new fidelity to the present signaled by the material he has used to repair the ruptured apparatus of flight: newspaper strips emblazoned in large print, 'The Times.' At last, George has aligned with the modern moment and its imperative to mend the rifts in the family. As the final production number, 'Let's Go Fly a Kite,' continues, George celebrates one's 'fist holding tight' no longer to the coinage of the capitalist realm but rather to the new, elevated perspective of the young. Mrs. Banks' contribution to the cause, the 'Votes for women' sash that she affixes as the kite's tail, has generally been perceived by critics as a relinquishment of feminist activism for a conventional gender role. However, although Winifred rejoins the family, the cause of women's liberation is perpetuated insofar as the sash becomes a high-flying protest banner, yet another in her successive acts of dual capitulation and subversion. In essence, she joins the feminist movement to the cause of widespread domestic and social reform.

If Disney's musical is to truly succeed in the project of cultural remediation, Poppins must become marginalized. After nursing the children in counterculturalism, she becomes an audience to her own inspiration, watching the reunified family through the frame of the nursery window as if viewing her own screened fantasy. The transition of domestic order appears complete insofar as not only does the public become devoted to the high-flying vision pursued by youth, but it is Michael who commands 'Now,' indicating to his father the appropriate moment of release [see Figure 5.6], followed by a close-up of the boy, then a long shot of the craft's elevating trajectory from his uplifted perspective. The 'now' as a moment of collectively embraced liberation from oppressive, dour groundedness is exhibited by citizens rallying together in joyous choral solidarity as they look skyward. Given *Poppins'* tropes, the scene bears resonances of adults turned on to another order of consciousness expansion to which youths in the 1960s were drawn. Considered a work of classical Hollywood cinema, in which the end replies to the beginning, no longer do the delinquent kite-chasing children pursue the experience of highness alone. In *Poppins'* uplifting final moments, during which the Bankses fly a kite in unison, a joyful resolution

Figure 5.6 An uplifting moment

seems to be achieved when the entire family (indeed the broader community) in essence becomes high together—an experience to which the audience is invited ('let's go') in song.

Nonetheless, there remain signs that the Banks culture is not altogether reformed. Bert once again upholds the capitalist system insofar as this gig worker, who Levin aptly characterizes as 'enterprising' (2007: 20), now sells kites to passersby. Further, although those who gather in solidarity bridge the generation gap, larger social reform has not been achieved. Class distinctions are maintained; with the exception of Bert, the lower stratum is absent from the picture. Moreover, in *Poppins*' nannying of the film audience, the scene bestows upon baby boomers suspicions about the patriarchal order, even if it manifests a certain attitudinal change. Despite the bank directors' uncommonly elevated moods while publicly participating in the latest trend, as the self-contained group flies kites (framed only as black-suited men pulling strings), there is no promise of an ameliorated system. It is certain that George's liberation from the bank will not last long. Encountering the gray-bearded Dawes Jr., who merrily reports that his father 'died laughing' from the earlier joke, George is appointed a bank partner, a position that he accepts from the string-pulling new chairman with utter gratitude. Inasmuch as the joke (which Dawes Jr. binds with ramifications in his sphere as a 'capital bit of humor') literally slayed the elder statesman of authoritarian economies, the ultimate effect has been that of creating an opening for George's accession to the boardroom. At the moment that George becomes enthusiastically committed to his family and freed from bureaucratic life, he is reeled in to a deeper partnership with the Establishment, whose new standard bearer avows no fundamental institutional change. The timeworn dominant order is thereupon not repudiated but rather guaranteed; George and the directors, for the moment able to appreciate alternate perspectives, remain tethered to longstanding capitalist culture.

Consequently, although the children's rebellion eventually proves so inspiring that it leads to would-be patriarchal change and uplifting mass harmony, troubling undercurrents remain not only for the diegetic world but also for Disney artistry. As cinema committed to displaying cultural betterment, Disney's musical remains entangled in its own struggles. Advancing a progressive agenda, *Poppins* yet remains committed to the circumvention of its extremist tendencies by moderating its discourse to appeal to mainstream audiences. This enterprising determination to recuperate domestic institutions forecloses the revolutionary transformations identified as central to addressing Poppins' dilemmas. Within the thematics of timeliness, the temporality of radical reform as an urgent yet fleeting cultural condition necessary to Disney as studio and cinema ultimately drives *Poppins*.

Poppins resists an unmitigated endorsement of counterculturalism while exhibiting the consequences. In the final scene, more comparable to a bank holiday than a revolution, Banks' rebellion is both endorsed and assured of suppression by the capitalist system via his encounter with the new bank chairman, who dually expresses appreciation of George's nonconformist humor (inducing the elder Dawes' pleasant, albeit by implication necessary, passing) and procures his partnership. The outcome guarantees that George's newfound commitment to the family will soon meet its own demise. In other words, the film ultimately asserts its status as a temporary fantasy. Before exiting skyward, Poppins affirms and advocates continuing suspicion of the patriarchal family. As she stands on the steps of the Banks home, a literal outsider to mainstream domesticity, her parrot-headed umbrella remarks that the children 'think more of their father than they do of you.' Poppins replies, 'That's as it should be.' Leaving the youths to a reconstituted paternal order, her remark indicates that their devotion to improved domestic conditions requires, as per the non-sentimental implication of the exchange, maintaining persistent vigilance over the patriarch.

Accordingly, Bert's wistful final remark, 'Goodbye Mary Poppins. Don't stay away too long,' followed by a reverse shot of Poppins turning her head and smiling down at him in acknowledgment, forewarns that the uplifted state of literal and figurative harmony, the apparent collective liberation from the confines of dominant imperialist culture, will be short-lived. Given the father's recommitment to and elevation in the capitalist order as bank partner in this production of the 1960s, together with the economic, aesthetic, and social imperatives imbuing *Poppins'* literary history and Disney cinema, the free-spirited commentator's farewell as the inspiring figure literally rises above constitutes the film's declaration that cultural reformation mobilized by a youth-oriented vision is temporary. Together with George's knee-jerk reversion to his original institution and Poppins' well-known returns to the family in Travers' series, Bert's sendoff bespeaks the impending deterioration of this euphoric ameliorated state and, correspondingly, anticipated film sequels.

George's final song, 'Let's Go Fly a Kite,' thereupon constitutes a form of lip service, cause for true revolution in the wake of his unhesitating abandonment of antiestablishmentarianism for a higher bank position. Consequently, the youths on- and off-screen are shown an illusion far darker than anything Poppins produces. In the larger picture, Disney offers an image of a transformed society joined together with its own critique, in other words, something for everyone. Insofar as Disney sells the revolution and its containment, the studio's investment in *Poppins* suggests a less-than-ideal vision. The ending is, accordingly, prescriptive, exhibiting how mainstream figures and institutions may appear to adopt new values but in reality subsume them in the reification of the prevailing order. Prefiguring the trajectory of 1960s youth resistance movements, radical cultural reform will eventually be foreclosed.

Consequently, if cultural remediation mobilized on the ground by the younger generation would seem to prevail in the closing scene, it is with ample warning of the Establishment's capacity to undermine radical change. Upon the conclusion, in the wake of *Poppins*' absence, baby boomers were liberated to the space outside the cinema not to rest on the laurels of an altogether jubilant ending, but rather in essence charged with a mandate to remain ever vigilant and wary of the father's order, however reformed it might appear to be. Invested with a consciousness-expanding vision—the inspiration that Poppins leaves in her wake as she rises to the ether—the children in the audience are left only with the option of looking up to an imaginary whose satisfaction might solely be possible by alighting on another Disney fantasy.

Costumed in the literal and figurative trappings of mass appeal, *Poppins* endorses a new order supported by a capitalist Establishment that, invested in the ethos of youth as opposed to only their value as successors to the patriarchy's economies, sets its sights for cultural advancement higher than that on which George and his superiors traditionally banked. In concert, *Poppins* acknowledges the constrictions of Disney cinema, the liabilities of what progressive youth culture risks in pursuing widespread (even multigenerational) popularity and developing a committed following. Such a vision embraces the project of creating a magnetizing liberation movement—signature escapist entertainment that, by rousing the imagination, inspires the general public. As a dramatic experience on- and off-screen, therapeutic as the film's movement would seem, at peril remains the compromise of its most elevating values in order to produce a reformed mainstream culture. The resulting gray area produced by the reemergent senior bankers and the succeeding final exchanges constitutes one upon which, by implication, the alightment of Disney's Poppins will again be unequivocally vital.

Notes

1 'Feed the Birds' so deeply appealed to Disney's sensibilities that it became his favorite song.
2 The performance aligns with stereotypical representations of overly joyful Black manual laborers.
3 Evincing their civility, with a doff of their caps the sweeps vacate the space of white bourgeois domesticity that they have temporarily occupied, addressing George as 'guv'nor.' This courteous titular acknowledgment of his superior

social status, lip service to the contravened order, constitutes a dual affirmation and containment of counterculturalism.

4 Associatively, escorting the runaway children home after counseling them on their father's travails, Bert sings, 'You might think a sweep's on the bottom-most rung ... In this whole wide world there's no happier bloke.' As Kenschaft observes, in this widely celebrated song ('Chim Chim Cher-ee') Bert 'insists that money and status have nothing to do with happiness' (1999: 234).

6 Reception
Changes in the Wind

Upon descending into movie theaters, *Mary Poppins* proved to be immensely popular with youths and a wealth of adults. Garnering top-grossing box office receipts that banked the studio more revenue than any previous release, 13 Academy Award nominations and five wins (see Introduction), numerous accolades for Julie Andrews in addition to an Oscar, and generally enthusiastic reviews, in essence Disney's fantasy was wholeheartedly embraced by many as the pinnacle of baby boomer cinema. Yet, much like George Banks' evaluation of Poppins, there remained some significant skepticism about the nature of the nanny's entertainment. Certain film critics, cultural commentators, and letter-to-the-editor writers reprimanded *Poppins* for its impact on youth sensibilities in respects not far removed from the screen patriarch's complaints: the subversion of longstanding cultural values. Paradoxically, in alignment with the film's thematic critiques of George's establishment, Disney's enterprise was rebuked for an overriding fidelity to capitalism that thwarted the production of a meritorious children's journey. The less-than-captivated pointed to Disney's unseemly spectacle of commercial imperialism in the form of a treacly adaptation (one, as noted by various detractors, accompanied by even more reductive product tie-ins), degrading the original literary series and, accordingly, the sensibilities of baby boomers. Consequently, albeit in general highly regarded as an uplifting modern classic, Disney's *Poppins* was judged by some as absolutely detrimental to youths' accession to the dominant cultural order. In neither case, however, was the film commonly recognized for the true modernity underlying such identifications.

The cultural conversation raised by *Poppins* and its influence were wide-ranging, in certain respects directly exhibiting contemporary tensions between the mainstream and counterculturalism. The young Andrews chafed under the constrictions of typecasting that produced her stardom and consequently threatened to corset her acting career. Caught in conflicts

DOI: 10.4324/9780429504600-7

between budding Hollywood fame and emancipation from its conventions—the embodiment of stereotypical femininity and liberation increasingly central to public discourse—Andrews both embraced and disinherited traditional gender roles on- and off-screen. Other elements of the film's determination by and investment in the radically changing times boldly surfaced in popular culture; *Poppins* was appropriated by some youth—and rebelliously endorsed by Andrews—as an icon of uninhibited trippiness. The film's impact extended to the vocabulary of the 1960s as well as popular music ranging from jazz to hard rock. Consequently, *Poppins* bridged traditionalism and contemporaneity, received as a present-day classic and a work of revitalizing newness. Amid this dynamic working its particular magic through the genre of youth cinema, *Poppins* evinced significant kinship to the teenpic as a work of cultural reanimation.

Enchantment

Poppins enraptured young baby boomers. Drawing a fervently devoted fan base, the musical became tantamount to a cult film. It was not unusual for children to see *Poppins* on multiple occasions, boast about numbers of viewings, and compare experiences. Director Todd Haynes recalled of *Poppins*, his first moviegoing experience,

> I was 3 years old and [...] *Mary Poppins* [...] made an impression on me that was seismic, apparently. I fell into some kind of total creative, imaginative rapture over that movie [...] just an obsessive, creative reaction to it.
>
> (quoted in Winslet 2011)

Although Haynes' parents were concerned about 'the hysteria I felt for this experience' (quoted in Lahr 2019: 52), the older generation, including cultural, educational, and social commentators largely endorsed *Poppins*, regarding the film as essential viewing for children.

Disney handsomely profited from such intense adoration. *Poppins* became the top-grossing film of 1965 according to *Variety* (because of its late-year release, the film reaped a smaller portion of its box office receipts in 1964).[1] In February of that year, the *Wall Street Journal* reported that Disney had logged 'record earnings in the first fiscal quarter [...] and officials told the annual meeting that fiscal 1965 profit would set a new high' ('Disney Had Record ...' 1965: 11). At the gathering, Irving Ludwig, president of Disney's distribution company, Buena Vista, announced that 'the total gross of *Mary Poppins* would be "two and a half times greater than any other Disney film and perhaps higher"' (ibid.). In March 1965, *Variety* reported that *Poppins'* estimated worldwide gross for the film was $40–50 million, a figure considered 'modest' insofar as hundreds of additional openings were scheduled ('"Mary Poppins" Ov ...' 1965: 14). Ludwig reported plans to 'keep "Mary Poppins" in active distribution as long as possible [...] due to high percentage of repeat customers' (ibid.). Capitalizing on *Poppins'* extraordinary allure, Disney rereleased the film the following year (1966). *Poppins* was thereby celebrated in Disney's own boardroom and hailed in Hollywood for the single-minded economic values eschewed by the film.

Reviewers were generally enchanted by *Poppins* as well. The film was deemed an instant classic, some suggesting that *Poppins* had assumed a place in the pantheon alongside *The Wizard of Oz* (Fleming, 1939).[2] The *NYT*'s Bosley Crowther pronounced the film 'a most wonderful, cheering movie' containing 'the enchantments of a beautiful production' (1964a: 34). The *Saturday Review*'s Hollis Alpert declared *Poppins* 'a burst of sheer frolicsome delight, one of the most magnificent pieces of entertainment ever to come from Hollywood' (1964: 22). John Coleman of England's *New Statesman* judged it Disney's 'tenderest, funniest and most ingenious production in years' (1964: 973). Those enthusiastic reviewers who addressed the issue of adaptation generally defended Disney's film from real or anticipated critiques. An uncredited *Newsweek* reviewer mused, 'The passionate devotees of P.L. Travers' *Mary Poppins* books may find Walt Disney musical version [...] an act of cultural vandalism. [...] They will be mistaken if they do' ('Julie, Julie' 1964: 112, 114). Reviews in the *NYT* and elsewhere noted the film's diegetic opposition to the status quo, including matters of gender roles, the patriarchal order, the institution of the family, and race—even if the timeliness of such representations and concerns was not distinguished. Crowther, for example, considered Poppins a woman of 'staunch individuality' with 'a look of complete authority' and 'the serenity of self-confidence,' one who 'vastly uplift[s] the spirits of that father-dominated family' (1964a: 35). During this moment of surging feminist consciousness, others perceived an archaic stereotype: a 'governess with witch-like powers' (Roud 1964: 9), a 'benevolent witch' (Rogers 1964: 2), while the self-proclaimed activist, Winifred, was dismissed.[3]

Similar to Travers' perception of her book series as one defying genre definitions that would limit its audience, Disney's *Poppins* was considered cinema possessing wide cross-generational appeal. *The Boston Globe*'s critic described the musical as 'a film basically designed for children [that] turns into enchanting magic for grown-ups as well' (Adams 1964: 18). Hedda Hopper pronounced that *Poppins* 'will live in the hearts of children from 7 to 70 forever' (1964: 18). Ironically, the prominent conservative newspaper *The Christian Science Monitor* signaled generational issues germane to 1960s tensions, specifically (and, it would seem, unwittingly) the value of rebellion against the status quo: 'The secret of […] [Poppins'] success […] is simply to make grownups act like children' (Rogers 1964: 2). At a historical moment when fractures between young and old were increasingly rending domestic and public life, *Poppins* was in essence celebrated for effectively bridging the generation gap.

The less enthralled critics excoriated *Poppins* for its lack of fidelity to Travers' classic and its conformity to the most reductive tendencies of children's cinema. Joyce Haber of the *Los Angeles Times* wrote, 'I found the Disney version utterly unfaithful to the original—saccharine, insipid, largely lacking in invention' (1967: C6). As will be discussed, such concerns were joined by those of academics and other cultural commentators who raised strong objections to the adaptation. Whereas reviewers almost invariably noted the film's excessive sugariness, most did not find it objectionable enough to ruin *Poppins* whereas others cringed. Certain reviewers critiqued the film for its disservice to youth in the form of inculcation not with higher, progressive values but vacuous tenets associated with conventional Disneyfication. *Newsday*'s reviewer wrote, 'the film qualifies on all fronts as ideal antiseptic entertainment. […] The story, typically Disney, is rife with empty homilies and depthless characterizations' (Cohn 1964a: C3). Consequently, for some who regarded the release an adulteration of a literary classic in the form of lightweight retrograde Disney classicism, elements of the film's modernity were unapparent. Yet others felt that the musical contained uncommon perceptivity as a genre film. Sensing perhaps an authentic immediacy in *Poppins*' focus on fractured bonds and new possibilities of solidarity, Coleman observed, 'Robert Stevenson has directed the complex revels with an affectionate feeling for human relationships quite unusual in this sort of enterprise' (1964: 974). As late as 2014, *Poppins* would be praised (by filmmaker Robert Greene) for its 'surprising emotional depth' (Greene 2014).

Although not perceived as a film that was shaped by or consequently addressed contemporary issues (including the oft-noted representation of Winifred as a suffragette), *Poppins* was viewed as a significant voice in 1960s culture battles in other regards. The musical was considered by some as an institutional bulwark against, or even an antidote to, the incursion of new screen styles characterized by hard-edged graphics and content, later described, in part, as the 'cinema of sensation' (Monaco 2001: 168). *Poppins* thereby became part of a larger conversation about the state of current cinema and issues of permissiveness troubling the cultural Establishment. Whereas *Newsday*'s reviewer harshly judged *Poppins* a categorically sanitized fantasy, others praised the film for this very quality, railing against the explicit violence and eroticism that progressively filled

American movie screens with a visceral new cinema appealing to younger (albeit not juvenile) audiences. Construing the film as a paragon of virtuous entertainment, some reviewers enlisted *Poppins* in the struggle for 'decent' youth cinema against a surge of early 1960s releases that stylistically and/or thematically reflected the changing cultural landscape. Such films included *Psycho* (Hitchcock, 1960), *Splendor in the Grass* (Kazan, 1961), *Lolita* (Kubrick, 1962), *The Manchurian Candidate* (Frankenheimer, 1962), and *Dr. Strangelove* (Kubrick, 1964).[4] Crowther wrote of *Poppins* and *My Fair Lady* (Cukor, 1964), 'In a medium which has lately been conspicuous for vulgarity, "sickness" and bad taste, two beautifully wholesome and refreshing entertainments have emerged' (1964b: X1). The *Baltimore Sun* praised the musical for a hygienic, untroubled purity: '"Mary Poppins" is [...] wholesome, happy and hearty. [...] During a week when the majority of the first-run theaters are showing movies about mental disease, adultery or multiple fornication, it is indeed refreshing to encounter one as consistently sunny and salubrious as [this film]' (Gardner 1965: 8). To such reviewers, Disney's latest construction of youth culture shielded cinema, and accordingly baby boomer audiences, from troubling modern sensibilities.

Yet, as classic Disney cinema, *Poppins* stirred up its own share of controversy. *Poppins* was deemed by some a film that challenged mainstream orthodoxies in deeply objectional respects. In the wake of *Poppins'* release, Disney was subject to significant criticism for abasing youth culture by bastardizing the children's classic through not only a syrupy musical adaptation but product tie-ins including highly adulterated, substandard book versions—all regarded as corrosive strategies of commercial imperialism.[5] The *NYT* reported, 'A Disney official said [...] that [*Poppins'*] total exploitation budget was "more than for any other picture" made by the company.' In conjunction, '38 licensees have been appointed by Disney to produce Mary Poppins merchandise' (Sloane 1964: 30). Consequently, whereas the film was almost universally praised for its cutting-edge technical ingenuity, particularly in the combined live-action and animation sequence, 'Jolly Holiday,' other modern techniques employed by Disney Productions were censured—those of commercialization.

Poppins became the flash point for a bitter struggle that soon erupted among educators over the state and stewardship of youth culture. In 1965, the *Los Angeles Times* published an article by California's Superintendent of Public Instruction, Dr. Max Rafferty, commending Disney cinema as a bastion of purity, virtue, and innocence within a sullied movie landscape. Characterizing Disney as 'the greatest educator of this century' (Rafferty 1965: A5), the conservative Rafferty explained, 'His live movies have become lone sanctuaries of decency and health in the jungle of sex and sadism created by the Hollywood producers of pornography' (ibid.). A strongly worded rebuttal addressed what was at stake for youths in the production of baby boomer cinema, attacking *Poppins* and other Disney adaptations for an extreme sanitization that presented its own radical challenges to the cultural order. In a letter to the *Los Angeles Times*, Frances Clark Sayers, retired children's librarian, author, and senior lecturer at UCLA, argued that Walt Disney had corrupted youth insofar as his work was responsible for the 'debasement of the traditional literature of childhood [...] manipulating and vulgarizing everything for his own ends. [...] The acerbity of Mary Poppins, unpredictable, full of wonder and mystery, becomes with Mr. Disney's treatment, one great marshmallow-covered cream puff' ('Walt Disney Accused' 1965: 602). She later observed, referring to the at least seven *Poppins* editions targeted to a spectrum of baby boomers (accounting for a significant quantity of the 25 million Disney books sold in the U.S. and abroad in 1964 [Bart and Bart 1965: BRA2]),

> I think Mr. Disney is basically interested in the market. He sees all this as a means of reaching a wider audience. [...] What I deplore [...] is his tendency to take over a piece of work and make it his own without any regard for the original author or to the original book. [...] it's a matter of merchandise with Mr. Disney. He is seeking that which sells quickly and easily to the mass market. What I deplore is that such books seem to show so little respect for the imagination of a non-reading child and so little respect for the capacity of a reading child.
>
> ('Walt Disney Accused' 1965: 604–605)

In this controversy over the value of Disneyfication, Sayers essentially aligned with the film's critique of capitalism-informed rhetoric creating internationally hegemonic cultural visions—an approach that, as underscored by *Poppins*, encompasses the disregard of children.

What Sayers and others denounced as Disney's acts of cultural imperialism raised additionally thorny issues that extended to the nurturance of youths as literal and figurative readers—and subjects—of culture as well as the constitution of youth culture through appropriation, conformity, and resistance. Critics railed against the corruption of children's aesthetic sensibilities, imagination, and intellect through the Disney books' 'sugary, over-glamorized style' (Bart and Bart 1965: BRA33) that, Sayers notes, 'consistently vulgarize illustration, oversimplify plot and limit vocabulary' (quoted in BRA2). Conversely, Disney was defended on the grounds that the books motivated children's educational and cultural development. Bart and Bart noted that the books

> present reading as some sort of 'good clean fun.' And though the books are [...] merchandising ploys [...] they also encourage many

nonreading children who've seen a Disney picture to pick up a book based on the film. Last of all, though the Disney books have, to a degree, mongrelized the classics, they have provided some rudimentary familiarity with aspects of these books and thus may encourage some children at a later date to take a look at the originals.

(BRA34)

Paradoxically, for those who perceived certain merits in Disney's adulteration of classics, the studio's culturally disobedient works constituted potential avenues for youths back to the literary canon.

Yet another important facet of the cultural conversation emphasized the imperatives of film adaptation for contemporary audiences. An interviewer asked Sayers, 'Are we making a distinction here between destroying or profaning something and simply modernizing it?' ('Walt Disney Accused' 1965: 608). From the vantage of his 1968 book, Richard Schickel, who initially observes, 'Disney's machine […] forc[es] everyone to share the same formative dreams' (18), later essentially lauds the timeliness of Poppins' screen representation as an 'independen(t),' 'nonconformist' 'model' for youths (348). Given the inscription of the historical context and the dramatic machinations necessary to construct mainstream youth cinema, by implication Schickel pictures the Technicolor Poppins as a valuably modern liberating inspiration for disquieted baby boomers, a characterization that yet acquiesces to additionally current cultural pressures of 'acceptab[ility].'

Julie Andrews: Problematic Captivation

Upon *Poppins'* release, Julie Andrews became the brightest star in Disney's— and, in many respects, Hollywood's—firmament. Widely celebrated for a magical performance in her film acting debut, Andrews won an Academy Award for Best Actress in a Leading Role, the only Disney film actress to date nominated in the category. Among other accolades, Andrews received a Golden Globe award for Best Actress, a BAFTA award for Most Promising Newcomer to Leading Film Roles (1965), and a Grammy for Best Recording for Children.[6] After debuting at #4 in the respected Quigley Publishing Company's 'Top Ten Money Making Stars Poll' of movie theater owners in 1965, Andrews rose to #1 in 1966 and 1967, topping Elizabeth Taylor and Doris Day. She was voted 'Star of the Year' by the Theater Owners of America and won the *Motion Picture Exhibitor* magazine's Golden Laurel Award for female musical performance in 1965 (and in 1966 for *The Sound of Music* [Wise, 1965]).[7] Yet, in accordance with the shifting cultural winds of the 1960s, Andrews' fidelity to her star image changed dramatically.

Initially, the press tended to portray Andrews as nearly a mirror image of Poppins: 'charming,' (Shipman 1966: 20, Tinee 1964: G11), 'pert, prim' (Bart 1964: X5), 'on the surface [...] all commonsense, levelheadedness, independence' (Shipman 1966: 20), 'angelic' (Cohn, 1964b: C3). Some celebrated Andrews as an ideal figure of youth. Hedda Hopper declared Andrews 'a young star of great loveliness' who 'looked like a teenager' (ibid.), and the *Boston Globe*'s critic noted, 'She sings with her own youthful enthusiasm' (Adams 1964a: 18). At the same time, issues of gender and domesticity shared center stage insofar as the media reported that Andrews was married and the mother of a baby when *Poppins* was in production. In the wake of *The Feminine Mystique*'s publication, and increasing feminist activism, those who profiled Andrews grappled with the tensions between traditional maternity and careerism, shifting between conventional and liberated images of the actress. Situating Andrews in a customary gender role off-screen, the press at first depicted her as a figure of domesticity who, albeit delighted with stardom, remained committed to home and family life as a new mother. In 1964, the *Christian Science Monitor* reported that while *The Sound of Music* was in production, Andrews was looking forward to 'the "heavenly chance" to settle in [her] new home and enjoy some family living' (Sammis 1964: 6). A 1965 Associated Press (AP) article published in the *Hartford Courant* with the headline 'Ironing Board Tipoff to Real Julie Andrews Behind Glamor Buildup' begins with the image of Andrews at a cherished English ironing board 'domestically propped up amid the chi-chi elegance of an opulent hotel suite': 'Filmdon's hottest star was about to press a party gown' (Glover 1965: 30A). The article proceeds to stress her unpretentious domestic nature, noting that Andrews answered her own telephone, 'quite possibly' holding her 2-year-old daughter (ibid.). In essence interrogating issues of modern womanhood, autonomy, and child-rearing that resonated with the roles of Poppins and Winifred Banks, numerous portrayals of Andrews' off-screen life described how she successfully yet with some difficulty negotiated motherhood and a consuming career as an independent 'single' woman insofar as she and her husband were separated (first by work, then by marital difficulties).

Consequently, 'Ironing Board' and other articles, such as 'Julie's Best Role: Homemaker' (Zylstra 1965: B12) and 'Julie Andrews Leads Flying Career as Star and Mother' (Sammis 1964: 6), pose a dilemma hovering behind the Disney musical. The AP reporter inquires 'Does she want to go on as a performer, or would she want to settle into less complicated domesticity?' and Andrews replies, 'If by some miracle one could do both without too much exhaustion, that would be perfect' (quoted in Glover 1965: 30A). In accordance, Andrews was depicted as an icon of young femininity, a fantasy figure not required to relinquish domesticity for careerism but rather

managing the two roles (albeit through the Hollywood 'magic' of her position as a well-compensated actress) and a realist who acknowledges that to
truly achieve such balance would be a 'miracle.' Essentially, she became a
mouthpiece for the necessity of *Poppins* as a feminist solution to the desires
of the modern woman independent of men. Exemplifying the cost of female
professional success, the following year Andrews was reportedly subject to
marital backlash for her stardom. *Time*'s 1966 cover story disclosed that she
and her husband, production designer Tony Walton, separated because he
'would not settle for a career of being Mr. Julie Andrews' ('The Now and
Future Queen' 1966: 57).[8]

Paradoxically, as an exemplar of certain feminist struggles in the
1960s, Andrews became most celebrated for two roles as nannies with
the 1965 release of *The Sound of Music*, another extraordinarily popular
film. Together, the roles shaped her screen persona as a young domestic
Other—employed by and committed to, but not of the family (initially, in
the case of *Music*)—a pure, inspiring iconoclast who liberates youth from
the old-fashioned, ironclad patriarchal order. In a 2000 essay, scholar Peter
Kemp recalled of viewing *Poppins* in his youth: 'Julie Andrews's per-
sonification of Mary Poppins and Maria von Trapp gave the child in me
panoramic insight into the self-liberating possibilities of orchestrated joy,
choreographed confidence and sung spirit' (56). However, Andrews' own
professional efforts at liberation were less than successful. If Poppins and
Maria are content in their roles as nannies, Andrews was decidedly not. In
Poppins' wake, Andrews embarked on a decades-long struggle to become
emancipated from the popular image of a wholesome nanny.

Andrews and co-star Dick Van Dyke implicitly became part of the public
conversation concerning child-rearing during a moment of anxiety about
the state of the nuclear family and the younger generation. Although her
image was a site of conflict regarding traditional and modern gender roles,
Andrews' dedication to her young daughter (unlike Winifred's maternal
conduct) was unquestioned. Together with the press on Van Dyke, in the
immediate wake of *Poppins'* release the two were depicted as exemplars
of parental fidelity coupled with mainstream family ideals, actors whose
presence alone would seem to rescue Hollywood from the menace of counterculturalism. Steven Watts observes, 'Both Julie Andrews, portrayed as
a devoted mother [...] and Dick Van Dyke, pictured as an ardent church-
goer and family man, were presented in national publications as paragons
of wholesome values' (2001: 408). As per the title of an *Austin Statesman*
column, the reviewer complained of 'Too Much Sex' on screen, celebrating
Poppins (as well as *My Fair Lady*) and Van Dyke's commitment to films
suitable for raising untarnished youth: 'Van Dyke's middle-western morals
[...] have caused him to turn down picture after picture which he wouldn't

want his four children to see him in' (Wilson 1964: 2). The actor's—and Bert's—images were underpinned by his popular small screen persona as charming, upstanding suburban family man Rob Petrie, a TV comedy head writer, in the hit sitcom *The Dick Van Dyke Show* (CBS, 1961–66). The witty, well-intentioned Midwest-born Petrie evinces certain liberal attitudes while affirming various conventional middle class values.

Initially acceding to the image of a spotless young woman devoted to domestic life, Andrews grew weary of her immaculate off-screen portrayal. She began to foreground her youthful affinity with liberation movements and other modern sensibilities, including free-spiritedness, countercultural defiance, and even trippiness. In a 1965 *Vogue* interview with future *Ms. Magazine* founder and feminist icon Gloria Steinem, Andrews groused, 'My problem [...] is that everybody thinks I'm a square' (124). A 1968 *Chicago Tribune* article begins, 'There's a rumor around Hollywood that the Julie Andrews mystique is undergoing a metamorphosis. Her marzipan image is changing' (Browning: 1968: 118). Andrews went so far as to lament to the interviewer, 'Crickey! I'm tired of playing bloody virgins' (ibid.). She was chronicled as a star struggling under the weight of mainstream Hollywood celebrity and consequently, in the wake of her biggest hits of the decade, pursuing roles calculated to avoid a career in which (as described by the reporter) she would be 'doomed to be typecast as a governess'—including the parts of war widow attracted to a morally dubious soldier and scientist engaged to, and engaging in premarital sex with, a colleague in the unpopular drama *The Americanization of Emily* (Hiller, 1964) and Cold War thriller *Torn Curtain* (Hitchcock, 1966), respectively. Nonetheless, 'thru them all her image remained [...] Miss Goody Two-Shoes, 100 percent pure Poppins' (ibid.). This reductive characterization of Poppins inhibited not only Andrews but recognition of the antiestablishmentarianism shared by the fictional figure and the actress. Indicating the decade's cultural tensions intersecting in the image of young women, as evinced in the representation of the female star, an 'intellectual-bachelor-hip-guru about town [Hollywood]' commented, '[Andrews is] a beautiful paradox. Part woman, part child, part independent feminist, part clinging vine' (quoted in Browning 1968: 119).

The most extreme rebellion against the sanitized image of Poppins/Andrews was mounted by members of the younger generation who celebrated the character's role as a supplier of trippy episodes. The figure of Poppins was publicly recirculated by some—and later endorsed by Andrews—as an agent of drug culture introducing on- and off-screen youths to the liberating euphoria of mind-bending experiences. Youth culture's appropriation of *Poppins* as a hallucinogenic film took the form of its own construction and distribution of popular images. By 1965, buttons and bumper stickers proclaimed 'Mary Poppins is a Junkie' [see Figure 6.1]. At the 1965 San Francisco International Film Festival, where Walt Disney received a Native Son award, an audience member asked his opinion of such bumper stickers; he replied, 'What's a junkie?' (Stein 2007). If Disney was not aware of the term (or deliberately feigned ignorance to maintain his image), Andrews was not so innocent. The star became complicit in circulating this countercultural image by sporting a 'Mary Poppins is a Junkie' bumper sticker on her car. Such interpretations did not escape all members of the older generation. In a 1966 *New Yorker* poem about a hospital patient on an IV, 63-year-old light verse poet Ogden Nash associated Poppins' work with that of administering a consciousness-altering pharmaceutical: 'Conveyer of morphia, the comforter [...] /Of sorcerers, vivisectionists, body-snatchers/Dr. Polyp is summoned [...]/[...] and Dr. Mary Poppins,/*La belle dame sans merci*' (Nash 1966: 30).[9] Mirroring its diegetic tensions, the film thereby became the site of a certain principally intergenerational struggle over the production of modern youth culture.

Largely marginalized—actually, ignored in film reviews as much as in their own home—were the children. Generally praising the performances but otherwise neglecting the siblings, reviewers' cursory accounts of the youths revealed resonantly conflicting points of view. Characterizations of the children diverged between figures of insubordination and tameness—'a pair of devils devoted to driving nannies to distraction' (Cohn 1964a: C3) to 'the most reasonable, the most well-behaved, the most wide-eyed young people you could possibly meet' (Adams 1964a: 18). Most reviewers keyed on the youths' attraction to Poppins' feats of unorthodoxy (e.g., 'The Banks children [...] are completely won over by Mary's tricks' [Hartung 1964:

Figure 6.1 Badge of the 1960s: Poppins as a figure of drug culture

24]). Yet, the children's original escapism, their desire for a transformed order, the necessity of their journey as one of inspired, newly liberated youths who through activism become agents of change, and the full consequences of their engagement were almost entirely overlooked in film critics' own captivation—both positive and negative—with Mary.

Vernaculars

Despite debates over *Poppins'* contributions or dangers to children's fantasy, the film not only spoke to baby boomers but disseminated youth culture in remarkably far-reaching ways. *Poppins* became a site of transmission from which the older generation absorbed, embraced, and adapted the culture of the young in respects that many would increasingly spurn as the decade wore on. The film's influence on mass culture extended to multiple vernaculars of the 1960s and beyond. *Poppins'* most psychedelic vocabulary, 'supercalifragilisticexpialidocious,' became assimilated into the general lexicon not only by youths but adults as well, initially employed in print by effusive reviewers describing the film and Andrews' performance. Consequently, the word was formally adopted by the linguistic Establishment; 'supercali...' was included in the 1966 *Random House Dictionary*. An index of how ingrained the adjective would become in popular speech and its continued association with an anticonservative sensibility, its usage as cultural commentary yet endures. Employing the term for political protest against the inauguration of a right-wing businessman as U.S. president, during the Women's March on Washington in January 2017 a protestor from a new generation held up a sign, 'SUPER CALLOUS FACIST RACIST EXTRA BRAGGADOCIOUS' [see Figure 6.2].

Poppins' modernity extended to certain unorthodox formal elements that would inspire future filmmaking. In a 2014 issue of *Sight & Sound*, documentary filmmaker Robert Greene described the film's 'truly radical narrative structure' and its influence on his work. Greene, who reported he had watched *Poppins* 'something like 37 times,' observed that *Poppins* defies the traditional 'over-determined' construction of fiction films. Instead, Greene noted, *Poppins'* composition is more akin to documentary cinema, 'built from captured moments that are by nature out of control' and 'priz[ing] frantic, unexpected moments over plot development' (Greene 2014). Although not perceived thusly by Greene, in such regards *Poppins* (awarded an Oscar for film editing) can be considered a youth film that structurally reflects the decade's liberation movements from conformism to the 'fixed and planned' by eschewing certain conventions of narrative cinema—one of numerous respects in which it constitutes a work of cultural reinvigoration through uplifting disengagement from the prevailing order.

Figure 6.2 A sign of *Poppins'* endurance in the lexicon of rebellion

The Sound of Music

Poppins' formidable cultural influence encompassed popular music. Heralded for a masterful film score, the Sherman brothers were awarded Oscars for Best Music and Best Original Song ('Chim Chim Cher-ee') as well as Grammys for Best Original Score Written for a Motion Picture and Best Recording for Children. The film was so popular among those in the music industry that in winning the Grammy for original score, *Poppins* bested the other 1964 youth musical that attracted an intensely devoted fan base, the Beatles' *A Hard Day's Night*, and the Disney soundtrack, which remained on *Billboard's* top ten chart for 48 weeks, was named the magazine's 1965 Album of the Year. *Variety* reported that more than 2.3 million *Poppins* soundtrack LPs had been sold by June 1966, with another 500,000 expected, and sales of two 'kiddy' records had reached more than 1.3 million copies—'an alltime high' for Disney's music division ('"Mary Poppins" Propels ...' 1966: 41).

 Poppins' impact on the musical landscape of the mid-1960s was something to sing about as well in that it extended to multiple generations and

styles. As of March 1965, music publisher Charles Hansen was market-
ing approximately 50 different arrangements of *Poppins* songs, 'from sheet
copies to [...] big band orchestrations' ('Cleffers ...' 1965: 74). Hansen
observed, 'It's far and away the biggest thing to hit the music business in
history' (ibid.). At the time, the *Poppins* soundtrack was the selling album
nationwide, a position it held on the *Billboard* charts for 14 weeks. *Poppins'*
captivating musical presence was felt not only in sales of Disney albums for
young listeners. The melodies significantly influenced adult music, embraced
by some of the most prominent musicians of the day. *Duke Ellington Plays
Mary Poppins* was released in 1965; the album was a collection of arrangements by the jazz legend and his collaborator, Billy Strayhorn. The back
cover explains the 'magic' of Poppins as a magnetic figure inspiring intergenerational and cross-cultural harmony, uniting disparate musical styles,
audiences, and musicians (Cornyn 1965). Yet another jazz musician, John
Coltrane, featured 'Chim Chim Cher-ee' as the top-billed song on his 1965
album *The John Coltrane Quartet Plays*. Incongruent as such attractions
may seem, jazz's stylistic liberation from traditional structure is simpatico
with *Poppins'* alternative values and construction.

Musical adaptations of *Poppins'* soundtrack, like the film, served a dual
cultural and commercial purpose in their crossover appeal to broader audiences. Disney's capitalization on *Poppins'* music became yet another reg-
ister of the studio's cultural imperialism. *Let's Fly With Mary Poppins*, a
1965 album produced by Disney's record subsidiary, Buena Vista, featured
vocals by popular Italian-American jazz singer Louis Prima and his wife,
Gia Maione. Two of the songs were sung not only in English but Italian for
the foreign market. Among other popular middle-aged entertainers who performed individual songs from the musical or recorded *Poppins* albums were
Bing Crosby, Burl Ives, and the Ray Coniff singers. Such appropriations of
popular youth culture for the capitalist purposes that motivated Banks in
effect transmitted Poppins' antiestablishment sensibility to the older generation through mainstream voices.

Poppins' soundtrack joined the chorus of socially conscious youth
music emerging in the early 1960s. Released at a time when young folk-
singers such as Bob Dylan, Joan Baez, and Peter, Paul, and Mary were
performing songs of social justice, *Poppins'* music had ties to the anthems
and singers of the young generation. In 1965, the same year that Barry
McGuire recorded his famed rendition of the 1964 antiwar anthem 'Eve of
Destruction,' he sang the lead vocals on the title track of The New Christy
Minstrels album *Chim Chim Cher-ee and Other Happy Songs*. Although
certainly less raw than McGuire's signature song, such *Poppins* numbers
attuned to the moment as 'Feed the Birds,' 'Sister Suffragette,' or the spirit
behind, e.g., the satirical 'Fidelity Fiduciary Bank' contributed to the new

music of social commentary and rebellion turning up the volume in the mid-1960s. Further, in at least one case, *Poppins*' harmonies seem to have influenced rock music. During a 2016 copyright infringement trial involving Led Zeppelin's 'Stairway to Heaven' (1971), *Poppins* became a significant presence in the courtroom. On the witness stand denying that the song's opening was poached from Spirit's 'Taurus' (1967), Zeppelin songwriter and guitarist Jimmy Page invoked the Disney musical. According to a Reuters article, Page 'was quicker to draw a comparison to "Chim Chim Cher-ee" in "Mary Poppins," when asked about a written declaration he gave for the lawsuit where he talked about "Stairway" and the more uptempo song from the Disney film' (Sinha-Roy 2016).[10]

Poppins' musical talents were recognized as an important and timely contribution to the art and industry of motion pictures. The film was heralded as a boon to cinema at a moment when box office receipts were continuing to decline in the wake of television's own magnetic draw. Articles in *Billboard*, the *NYT*, and *Variety* touted *Poppins* (and other musicals, including Andrews' *The Sound of Music*, *My Fair Lady*, and *A Hard Day's Night*) as films that were revivifying Hollywood through the renewal of the genre. A report in *Variety* was headlined, 'Cleffers Rejoice as "Poppins," "Hoods" Hint Return of Orig H'wood Filmusicals' (1965: 74).[11] The *Times*' Crowther observed that *Poppins* and *My Fair Lady* 'more or less held the ground achieved by "West Side Story" (at least, they have shown such style and grace that they cannot be charged with retrogressing)' (1965: X1). *Billboard* paraphrased an observation by musical score writer Ervin Drake: 'the movie musical [such as *Poppins* and *Sound of Music*] can be Hollywood's definitive answer to the problems presented by TV competition over the past decade' (Gross 1965: 12). Richard Schickel, too, considered *Poppins* a reinvigoration of the genre, noting that the 'Jolly Holiday' and 'Chim Chim Cher-ee' sequences

> have a cinematic excitement entirely missing from most film musicals of recent years and far in advance—as the whole film is—of something like *The Sound of Music*, to which it is superior musically, directorially, thespically and even intellectually.
>
> (1968: 357)

Albeit perceived as a film for young baby boomers, *Poppins* worked a significant amount of its magic through conventions of cinema produced for older youths. As a genre film, *Poppins* challenged categorical divisions among youth releases insofar as it exhibits significant ties to the teenpic. Specifically, in concert with key musical teenpics, *Poppins* ultimately works its particular magic of would-be cultural remediation through an ultimately

infectious counterculturalism that reanimates an exhausted patriarchal society—albeit with significant caveats and looming dangers. Akin to such
musical teenpics as *Rock Around the Clock* (Sears, 1956) and *A Hard Day's
Night*, through youth-allied outsider music, moribund Establishment-bound
culture becomes revitalized and reconstituted. In this unexplored connection
between *Poppins* and musicals for older members of the young generation,
revolutionary changes take place through music, constituting a metaphor
for transformation through the choral voices of a rejuvenating sensibility.

Harmonizing with certain unorthodox youth cinema of its day, *Poppins*
shares affinities with the other London-set episodic musical of 1964 that
became a cultish hit: *A Hard Day's Night*. Both are films involving mind-
bending experiences that take place within (albeit very different) spaces
of realism, displaying tensions of the generation gap, irreverence toward
longstanding institutions, multiple registers of escapism, and baby boomers' magnetic attraction to a single or multiple singing twenty-somethings,
captivating entertainers who are mouthpieces for the yearnings of youth. In
each film, wherein the younger generation resists a staid patriarchal culture,
the celebrated figures of rebellion undermine the Establishment through
superior wit and verbal skills. Albeit outsiders, they form cobbled-together
young families with and to whom they communicate embracing musical
messages (more socially conscious on the part of *Poppins*). Celebrating a
freeing trippiness, their enthralling presence magically unhinges and alters
the dominant order. In certain regards, *Poppins'* escapist journey looks ahead
to, if not paves the way for, the liberating, consciousness-expanding excursions of *Easy Rider*. The 1969 social statement about the consequences of
an outdated militaristic power structure is constructed as another episodic,
music-laden plot overlain on a slim narrative thread, in which members of
the younger generation embark on mind-bending adventures. The escapist
journey through multiple social classes, conditions, and forms of trippiness
exhibits how countercultural experiences bring necessary, albeit ultimately
unsustainable, peace of mind.

Poppins' central importance as 1960s youth cinema ultimately lies in the
cultural consciousness that transcends its genre. The film's loudly voiced
concerns about the times and its multiple rebellions against the status quo
comprise a spectrum of resonant domestic and social issues that exceed
(with some exceptions, e.g. *West Side Story*) children's or youth-centered
musicals of its day. In certain respects, Disney's fantasy proves more akin
to such diagnostic youth-focused non-musicals as the foundational teenpic *Rebel Without a Cause* and *Compulsion* (Fleischer, 1959), neither of
which celebrate the young but rather focus on identifying the failings of the
older generation and its rigidly deterministic order which produces troubled youth. Such films ushered in *To Sir, With Love* (Clavell, 1967) and

The Graduate, among other sober 1960s releases. Yet, as opposed to such cinema, *Poppins* indoctrinates young baby boomers in not only the concerns but possibilities of their generation and enlightens their elders in the values of oppositional youth culture. This forward-looking baby boomer cinema does not shrink from critiquing a society constraining youths and parents, the outmoded institutions and allegiances to stultified domestic life that must be relinquished (at least for a time) to a young caregiver with an uplifting cultural vision at a moment of urgency, fulfilling the need among children and adults for liberation and inspiring youth activism that results in measures of reform. In sum—whether despite or given the ultimate troubling embrace of a renewed patriarchal capitalist order, implying the necessary return of a magically elevating sight—*Poppins* constitutes a manifesto of the powers of youth cinema itself.

Notes

1 *Poppins* was rereleased in 1966 and at various intervals through 2020 (as of this writing) for a cumulative worldwide gross of $103 million, according to IMDb. In addition to its theatrical releases, the film has been distributed in VHS, laserdisc, and DVD formats, as well as through video on demand.
2 See in particular Smith (1964: 25) and Alpert (1964:22).
3 Winifred was roundly judged (and still debated) as a figure who undermines her own militant dedication to equality: e.g., 'a scatter-brained battler for women's rights' (Cohn 1964a). Reviewers noted that she not only readily capitulates to her husband but bears significant responsibility for the children's rebelliousness by her 'neglect' (Cohn; Smith 1964: 24).
4 The shift would culminate in such late-decade films as *Bonnie & Clyde* (Penn, 1967) and *Easy Rider* (Hopper, 1964).
5 Other product tie-ins included albums, 'easy piano' sheet music, dolls, and coloring books.
6 The last award was shared with the Sherman Brothers, musical arranger and conductor Irwin Kostal, and Dick Van Dyke.
7 She also received Golden Laurels for Top Female Star in 1967 and 1968.
8 Andrews and Walton, *Poppins*' production designer, divorced in 1967.
9 The French phrase refers to an 1819 Keats poem wherein a medieval knight meets a 'supernatural' character 'sing[ing]/A faery's song' and transporting him to an 'illusory world.'
10 '"I may have said the chord sequences are very similar because that chord sequence has been around forever," Page said' (Sinha-Roy 2016).
11 'Hoods' refers to *Robin and the Seven Hoods* (1964).

Coda
Poppins Redux

If Disney's *Mary Poppins* enjoyed a largely spotless reputation in 1964, the character's future in the entertainment business would be considerably more checkered. After abandoned attempts by the Disney company, Travers, and others to bring Poppins to cinema, television, and the stage in the 1980s (Lawson 2013: 347–351), the nanny's return remained deferred until Disney Theatrical Productions mounted a hugely successful stage adaptation (based on the film and second *Poppins* book) that opened in London and on Broadway in 2004 and 2006, respectively. It would be 50 years until Poppins returned to the screen, taking the form of two variably received releases. Despite their mixed receptions, Disney's *Poppins* origin story, *Saving Mr. Banks* (2013), and second visitation of the nanny at a moment of crisis, *Mary Poppins Returns* (2018), addressed some significant unfinished business. In succession looking inward and outward, the latter Disney films produced their own cinema of awareness devoted to recurring issues of cultural consciousness.

Saving Mr. Banks dramatizes *Poppins'* screen adaptation, particularly the fraught relationship between Travers and Walt Disney as the mogul and his creative team attempt to sell the studio's fantasy to the author, who is loath to relinquish her original vision to Disney's concept and style of youth cinema. This interior view of the challenging process of transliterating past fantasy into present-day material for children and family audiences through a signature studio 'system' combines a backstage musical with flashbacks to Travers' girlhood and Poppins' roots. Conversely, *Returns*, like its 1964 predecessor, regards the broader cultural conditions that necessitate Mary's appearance, reflecting a present-day historical moment in which magical intervention and release from the day's grave troubles were perceived by a great many as categorical necessity and absolute fantasy. By implication, even the heeded lessons of *Poppins'* 1960s have not produced a redeemed culture that guarantees the original film's youth a life lived happily ever after.

DOI: 10.4324/9780429504600-8

In the sequel *Mary Poppins Returns*, the nanny again visits a domestic world in the throes of catastrophe. Set amid, per the opening frames, 'The Great Slump' (as is the original book, although Travers does not specify the Depression), the cause of disorder is soon singled out as a moneyed man given to dangerously false pretenses, an antagonist obsessed with financial gain through shady real estate acquisitions: Wilkins (Colin Firth), the deceitful, swindling president of Fidelity Fiduciary Bank. Poppins (Emily Blunt) arrives at a critical time, when the Banks family is on the precipice of losing the family home to repossession, a burdensome prevailing order heavily borne from the start by melancholy patriarch Michael (Ben Whishaw), now a widower with three children, and his sister, Jane (Emily Mortimer). In this fable released midway through the tumultuous presidency of an autocratic American real estate developer consumed by economic accumulation and well known for making self-serving, mendacious statements and violating the law, domestic conditions are so dire that the man fixated on the acquisition of the Banks home must himself be foreclosed upon, with the magical aid of Poppins in a cultural fantasy of the 2010s. Foregrounding the allegorical nature of the film, whose main plot is not adapted from Travers, *Returns'* central production number, 'A Cover Is Not the Book,' features the quadruply repeated line, 'under the covers one discovers that the king may be a crook.'

The film is rife with nods to its predecessor that contain an associated cultural consciousness. Michael is not a figure of the economic patriarchy but victim of it. A painter who must work as a bank teller to support the family, he is an individual essentially produced by the original musical and the ethos of the 1960s, as is his sister. Michael is an artist and gentle, understanding father who does not buy into the bank. Jane is a social activist at the Society for the Protection of the Rights of the Underpaid Citizens of England, fighting for equality and compassion for commoners depreciated by proprietors of the capitalist system. More racially and ethnically diverse, *Returns* contains a sprinkling of multicultural casting, characteristic of modern Disney cinema. Playing the male lead—Bert-like perpetually upbeat lamplighter Jack—Lin-Manuel Miranda, an American of Puerto Rican and Mexican descent, lends not only cultural inclusiveness but, as renowned writer and star of the hit 2015 play *Hamilton*, an association with capitalism-linked drama.[1] Black lawyer Frye (Kobna Holdbrook-Smith) is the sole bank employee sympathetic to Michael's plight. Nonetheless, near economic disaster is set to rights by portrayer of the original Bert and bank chairman Dawes, Senior—actor Dick Van Dyke—who surfaces as retired bank director Dawes, Junior to fire his grasping nephew Wilkins. The unsugary returning Poppins plays a less countercultural role, leading the more enlightened and responsible Banks youths to recuperate their childhood through flights of the imagination and otherwise turning back time.

In *Returns'* happy ending, like its 1964 predecessor, successive knocks on the bank ultimately give way to a jaundiced reendorsement. The rescue of the Banks home from foreclosure hinges on recovering valuable shares of bank stock acquired by George Banks through investing young Michael's tuppence, sign of the remedial power of well-intentioned capitalist economics. The final production number, 'Nowhere to Go But Up' captures the cultural mood of millions that would reach its apotheosis in the 2020 American presidential elections. Yet, this forcibly optimistic film, signaling the production's bleak times, closes with an air of lost hope. Against the backdrop of momentary joy in recovering the family home, Poppins' return cannot be anticipated or even wished for. The 2018 *Poppins* concludes with a certain abandonment of confidence in 'saving' that has theretofore sustained Disney. Bereft of such sentiments as 'don't stay away too long' expressed upon the nanny's original departure, the sequel suggests that, given the state of domestic culture in the latter 2010s, Poppins' return to resolve future domestic chaos no longer constitutes even the stuff of fantasy.

Note

1 Walt Disney Pictures produced a 2020 film based on the play.

Bibliography

Adams, M. (1964) 'Walt Disney's "Mary Poppins" Proves Magic for Children and Grown-Ups,' *Boston Globe*, 23 October, p. 18.

'All-Time Top Grossers' (1966) *Variety*, 5 January, p. 6.

Alpert, H. (1964) 'Mary Poppins to the Rescue,' *Saturday Review*, 22 August, p. 22.

Baker, R. (1999) 'A Writer Worth Her Salt,' in E. Draper and J. Koralek (eds.), *A Lively Oracle: A Centennial Celebration of P.L. Travers, Creator of Mary Poppins*, Burdett, NY: Larson Publications, pp. 120–32.

Bart, P. (1964) 'The Hollywoodization of Julie Andrews: Broadway's Fairest Lady Becomes A Movie Star Three Times Over,' *New York Times*, 6 September, p. X5.

Bart, P. and Bart, D. (1965) 'As Told and Sold by Disney,' *New York Times*, 9 May, pp. BRA2, 32–4.

Bergsten, S. (1978) *Mary Poppins and Myth*, Stockholm: Almqvist & Wiksell.

Bettelheim, B. (1962) 'The Problem of Generations,' *Daedalus*, Vol. 19, No. 1, Winter, pp. 68–96.

'Big Rental Pictures of 1965' (1966) *Variety*, 5 January, p. 6.

Brode, D. (2004) *From Walt to Woodstock: How Disney Created the Counterculture*, Austin, TX: University of Texas Press.

Browning, N. (1968) '"Crickey! I'm Tired of Playing Bloody Virgins",' *Chicago Tribune*, 1 September, pp. 118–19.

Buell, E. (1958) 'For 9–12: The Magic Realm of Fantasy,' *New York Times*, 2 November, BRA, p. 30.

Burness, E. and Griswold, J. (1982) 'P.L. Travers, The Art of Fiction No. 63,' *The Paris Review*, Vol. 24, No. 86, Winter, pp. 210–29.

Carter, D. (2018) 'Literary, But Not Too Literary; Joyous, But Not Jazzy: *Triad Magazine*, Antipodean Modernity and the Middlebrow,' *Modernism/Modernity*, Vol. 25, No. 2, April, pp. 245–67.

Chamberlain, J. (1934) 'Books of the Times,' *New York Times*, 3 December, p. 15.

'Cleffers Rejoice as "Poppins," "Hoods" Hint Return of Orig H'wood Filmusicals' (1965) *Variety*, 24 March, p. 74.

Coleman, J. (1964) 'Julie Poppins,' *New Statesman*, 1 July, pp. 973–4.

Cohn, A. (1964a) '"Mary Poppins" A Nanny Nobody Can Figure Out,' *Newsday*, 25 September, p. C3.

Cohn, A. (1964b) 'Julie Likes Being a Lady—Within Reason,' *Newsday*, 16 September, p. C3.

Cornyn, S. (1965) 'Liner Notes,' *Duke Ellington Plays Mary Poppins*, Reprise Records (recorded 1964).

Corona, J. (2021) 'His Vaccine Story Inspired His Father to Write a Disney Classic,' *Morning Edition*, NPR, 8 January. https://www.npr.org/2021/01/08/954413533/his-vaccine-story-inspired-his-father-to-write-a-disney-classic.

Crowther, B. (1964a) 'Screen: "Mary Poppins",' *New York Times*, 25 September, p 34.

Crowther, B (1964b) 'Welcoming Two Fair Ladies,' *New York Times*, 25 October, pp. X1, X9.

Crowther, B. (1965) 'What's Score Now in Musical Films?' *New York Times*, 7 March, p. X1.

Cuomo, C. (1995) 'Spinsters in Sensible Shoes: *Mary Poppins* and *Bedknobs and Broomsticks*,' in E. Bell, L. Haas and L. Sells (eds.), *From Mouse to Mermaid: The Politics of Film, Gender, and Culture*, Bloomington, IN: Indiana University Press, pp. 212–23.

Darrow, Jr., W. (1968) 'Cartoon,' *New Yorker*, 24 August, p. 36.

Davidson, B. (1964) 'The Fantastic Walt Disney,' *Saturday Evening Post*, 7 November, pp. 67–8, 71, 74.

'Disney Had Record Net in First Fiscal Quarter' (1965) *Wall Street Journal*, 3 February, p. 11.

'Disney's Live-Action Profits' (1965) *Business Week*, 24 July, pp. 78–82.

Doherty, T. (2002) *Teenagers and Teenpics: The Juvenilization of American Movies in the 1950s*, 2nd Edition, Philadelphia, PA: Temple University Press.

Everett, A. (2008) '1961: Movies and Civil Rights,' in B.K. Grant (ed.), *American Cinema of the 1960s: Themes and Variations*, New Brunswick, NJ: Rutgers University Press, pp. 44–66.

Flanagan, C. (2005) 'Becoming Mary Poppins: P.L. Travers, Walt Disney, and the Making of a Myth,' *New Yorker*, 19 December, pp. 40–6.

Fox, M. (1996) 'P.L. Travers, Creator of the Magical and Beloved Nanny Mary Poppins, is Dead at 96,' *New York Times*, 25 April, p. B14.

Frankel, H. (1964) 'A Rose for Mary Poppins,' *Saturday Review*, 7 November, No. 47, pp. 24–5, 57.

Friedan, B. (1963) *The Feminine Mystique*, New York: Norton and Company.

Gabler, N. (2006) *Walt Disney: The Triumph of the American Imagination*, New York: Alfred Knopf.

Gardner, R.H. (1965) '"Mary Poppins",' *Baltimore Sun*, 16 January, p. 8.

Glover, W. (1965) 'Ironing Board Tipoff to Real Julie Andrews Behind Glamor Buildup,' *Hartford Courant* (AP), 14 February, p. 30A.

Gitlin, T. (1993) *The Sixties: Years of Hope, Days of Rage*, New York: Bantam Books (originally published in 1987).

Goodman, P. (2012) *Growing Up Absurd*, New York: New York Review Books (originally published in 1960).

Greene, R. (2014) 'Find the Fun: Editing Documentaries the Mary Poppins Way,' *Sight & Sound*, online, 22 January, https://www.bfi.org.uk/news-opinion/sight

-sound-magazine/comment/unfiction/find-fun-editing-documentaries-mary
-poppins-way.

Gross, M. (1965) 'B'way's Songwriters Could be Hollywood Cure-All: Drake,' *Billboard*, 17 April, p. 12.

Haber, J. (1967) 'Where Reviewers, Audiences don't Agree,' *Los Angeles Times*, 31 December, p. C6.

Hartung, P. (1964) 'Mary Poppins,' *Teacher Edition of Senior Scholastic*, 21 October, p. 24.

Helping Teenagers Explore Values: A Resource Unit for High School Teachers (1956) Columbus, OH: Ohio State University Press.

Hopper, H. (1964) 'Disney's "Mary Poppins" Wins Praise,' *Chicago Tribune*, 29 August, p. 18.

Jackson, P. (2012) *Great War Modernisms and The New Age Magazine*, London: Continuum.

Johnson, T. (1999) 'Journeyer Back to Here and Now,' in E. Draper and J. Koralek (eds.), *A Lively Oracle: A Centennial Celebration of P.L. Travers, Creator of Mary Poppins*, Burdett, NY: Larson Publications, pp. 133–43.

'Julie, Julie' (1964) *Newsweek*, 5 October, pp. 112, 114.

Kennedy, J. (1963) 'CBS Evening News: Interview by Walter Cronkite,' September 2.

Kemp, P. (2000) 'How Do You Solve a "Problem" Like Maria von Poppins?' in B. Marshall and R. Stillwell (eds.), *Musicals—Hollywood and Beyond*, Exeter: Intellect Books, pp. 55–61.

Kenschaft, L. (1999) 'Just a Spoonful of Sugar? Anxieties of Gender and Class in "Mary Poppins",' in B. Clark and M. Higgonet (eds.), *Girls, Boys, Books, Toys: Gender in Children's Literature and Culture*, Baltimore, MD: Johns Hopkins University Press, pp. 227–42.

Kohler, C. (1968) 'Stanley Kubrick Raps,' *The Eye*, August, pp. 30, 84–6.

Lahr, J. (2019) 'The Director's Cut,' *New Yorker*, Vol. 95, No. 35, 11 November, p. 52.

Lawson, V. (2013) *Mary Poppins, She Wrote: The Life of P.L. Travers*, New York: Simon & Schuster (originally published in 1995 under the title *Out of the Sky She Came* by Hodder).

Levin, D. (2007) 'The Americanization of *Mary*: Contesting Cultural Narratives in Disney's *Mary Poppins*,' in L. Stratyner and J. Keller (eds.), *Fantasy Fiction Into Film: Essays*, Jefferson, NC: McFarland and Co., pp. 115–23.

'Mary Poppins' (1962) *New Yorker*, 20 October, pp. 44–5.

'"Mary Poppins" Ov $11-Mil, Domestic' (1965) *Variety*, 24 March, p. 14.

'"Mary Poppins" Propels Disney Music Div. to Alltime $9,000,000 Gross' (1966) *Variety*, 29 June, p. 41.

Mary Poppins Special Edition CD (2004) Walt Disney Records.

McBride, J. (1977) 'Stevenson Preps His 20th Disney Film in 21 Years,' *Variety*, 14 July, pp. 1, 11.

McDonald, R. (2014) 'The Irish Revival and Modernism,' in J. Clearly (ed.), *The Cambridge Companion to Irish Modernism*, New York: Cambridge University Press, pp. 51–62.

McGilligan, P. (1978) 'Who is the World's Most Successful Director?' *American Film*, Vol. 3, No. 5, 1 March, pp. 20–6.

McLeer, A. (2002) 'Practical Perfection? The Nanny Negotiates Gender, Class, and Family Contradictions in 1960s Popular Culture,' *National Women's Studies Association Journal* Vol. 14, No. 2, Summer, pp. 81–101.

Mead, M. (1960) 'What Makes Women Unhappy?' *Chatelaine* Vol. 33, No. 3, March, pp. 25, 44, 46, 48–9.

Mitchell, J. (2005) 'Jim Stark's "Barbaric Yawp": *Rebel Without a Cause* and the Cold War Crisis in Masculinity,' in J.D. Slocum (ed.), *Rebel Without A Cause: Approaches to a Maverick Masterwork*, Albany, NY: SUNY Press, pp. 131–47.

'Military Advisors in Vietnam: 1963' (n.d.) John F. Kennedy Presidential Library and Museum, https://www.jfklibrary.org/learn/education/teachers/curricular -resources/high-school-curricular-resources/military-advisors-in-vietnam-1963.

Monaco, P. (2001) *History of the American Cinema: The Sixties*, New York: Charles Scribner's Sons.

Nash, O. (1966) 'Notes for the Chart in 306,' *New Yorker*, 25 June, p. 30.

'New English Weekly' (1932) Time magazine Vol. 19, No. 20, 16 May, p. 35.

Newquist, R. (1967) 'P.L. Travers,' in *Conversations*, Chicago, IL: Rand McNally & Co., pp. 423–33.

O'Brien, F. (1937) *An Invitation to Read: The Use of the Book in Child Guidance*, New York: Municipal Reference Library.

Oliver, P. (2014) *Hinduism and the 1960s: The Rise of a Counter-Culture*, London: Bloomsbury.

Paglia, C. (2003) 'Cults and Cosmic Consciousness: Religious Vision in the American 1960s,' *Arion*, Vol. 10, No. 3, Winter, pp. 57–111.

'Pamela Travers' (1924) *The Triad*, Vol. 9, No. 4, 11 February, p. 36.

Parker, M. (2015) 'Richard M. Sherman Interview: The Legendary Disney Songsmith's Extraordinary Life,' *Smashing Interviews Magazine*, online, 30 July, http://smashinginterviews.com/interviews/musicians/richard-m -sherman-interview-the-legendary-disney-songsmiths-extraordinary-life.

Pogash, C. (2014) 'At Berkeley, Free (Though Subdued) Speech, 50 Years Later' *New York Times*, 1 October, pp. A18.

Pollack-Pelzner, D. (2019) '"Mary Poppins," and a Nanny's Shameful Flirting With Blackface,' *New York Times*, 28 January, p. C1.

President's Commission on the Status of Women (1963) *American Women: Report of the President's Commission on the Status of Women*, Washington, DC: U.S. Government Printing Office.

Pryor, T. (1968) 'Year of Fevers: Merger Mania, Lost Jobs, Classification,' *Daily Variety, 35th Anniversary Edition*, 29 October, pp. 8–10.

'Quick, Go Get Dr. Spock!' (1962) *Life* magazine, 14 December, pp. 90A, 90B, 92.

Rafferty, M. (1965) 'The Greatest Pedagogue of All,' *Los Angeles Times*, 19 April, p. A5.

Ramsey, E. (ed.) (1937) *Reading for Fun: For Boys and Girls in the Elementary School*, Chicago, IL: The National Council of Teachers of English.

Roesch, R.F. (1962) 'Generation Gap Affects Parent-Child Relations,' *Daily Record*, The Stroudsburgs, PA, 28 July, p. 6.

Rogers, H. (1964) '"Mary Poppins" On Screen,' *Christian Science Monitor*, 3 November, p. 2.

Roud, R. (1964) 'New Films in London,' *Guardian*, 18 December, p. 9.

Sammis, C. (1964) 'Julie Andrews Leads Flying Career as Star and Mother,' *Christian Science Monitor*, 12 October, p. 6.

Schickel, R. (1968) *The Disney Version*, New York: Simon & Schuster.

Scholes, R. (n.d.) 'General Introduction to *The New* Age 1907–1922,' *Modernist Journals Project*, online, https://modjourn.org/general-introduction-to-the-new-age-1907-1922-by-scholes-robert/.

Sherman, Robert (2013) *Moose: Chapters From My Life*, Bloomington, IN: AuthorHouse.

Sherman, R. and Sherman, R. (1998) *Walt's Time: From Before to Beyond*, Santa Clarita, CA: Camphor Tree Publishers.

Shipman, D. (1966) 'The All-Conquering Governess,' *Films and Filming*, August, pp. 16–20.

Sibley, B. (1999) 'How Are They Going to Make *That* into a Musical?' in E. Draper and J. Koralek (eds.), *A Lively Oracle: A Centennial Celebration of P.L. Travers, Creator of Mary Poppins*, Burdett, NY: Larson Publications, pp. 51–62.

Silverman, D. and Silverman, O. (2016) '"This is Not the Mary Poppins I Know!": P.L. Travers Goes to Hollywood,' in D. Brode and S. Brode (eds.), *It's the Disney Version!: Popular Cinema and Literary Classics*, New York: Rowman & Littlefield, pp. 141–50.

Simons, J. (2000) 'Spectre Over London: *Mary Poppins*, Privatism and Finance Capital,' *Scope: Online Journal for Film and Television Studies*, July, https://www.nottingham.ac.uk/scope/documents/2000/july-2000/simons.pdf.

Sinha-Roy, P. (2016) 'Led Zeppelin's Page Testifies to "Stairway" and "Mary Poppins" Song Similarity,' *Reuters*, 16 June, https://www.reuters.com/article/us-music-ledzeppelin-idUSKCN0Z21A5.

Sloane, L. (1964) 'Advertising: Mary Poppins Fad Designed,' *New York Times*, 24 July, p. 30.

Solnit, R. (2006) 'Three Who Made a Revolution,' *The Nation*, online, 16 March, https://www.thenation.com/article/archive/three-who-made-revolution/.

Smith, L. (1964) "Fantasies on the Ceiling," *Cosmopolitan*, Vol. 157, No. 5, November, pp. 24–5.

Smulders, S. (2014) '"We are All One": Money, Magic, and Mysticism in *Mary Poppins*,' in A. Hubler (ed.), *Little Red Readings: Historical Materialist Perspectives on Children's Literature*, Jackson, MI: University of Mississippi Press, pp. 78–91.

Spock, B. (1946) *The Common Sense Book of Baby and Child Care*, New York: Duell, Sloane and Pearce.

Stein, R. (2007) '50/San Francisco International Film Festival/Shirley Temple Packs a Wallop,' *SFGATE*, online, 9 March, https://www.sfgate.com/entertainment/article/50-SAN-FRANCISCO-INTERNATIONAL-FILM-FESTIVAL-2578386.php.

Steinem, G. (1965) 'Julie Andrews,' *Vogue*, Vol. 145, No. 6, pp. 124–5, 154.

Stevenson, A. (2018) '"Cast Off the Shackles of Yesterday": Women's Suffrage in Walt Disney's *Mary Poppins,*' *Camera Obscura,* Vol. 33, No. 2, pp. 69–103.

Stewart, R. (ed.) (2010) *American Military History, Vol. II,* second edition, Washington, DC: Center of Military History, U.S. Army.

Stewart, S. (2013) 'Disney Trashes 'Poppins' Author in "Saving Mr. Banks",' *New York Post,* online, 8 December, https://nypost.com/2013/12/08/disney-trashes -poppins-author-in-saving-mr-banks/.

Students for a Democratic Society (1962) *Port Huron Statement,* online, http:// www2.iath.virginia.edu/sixties/HTML_docs/Resources/Primary/Manifestos/ SDS_Port_Huron.html.

Swerdlow, A. (1993) *Women Strike for Peace: Traditional Motherhood and Radical Politics in the 1960s,* Chicago, IL: University of Chicago Press.

Szumsky, B. (2000) '"All That is Solid Melts into the Air": The Winds of Change and Other Analogues of Colonialism in Disney's *Mary Poppins,*' *The Lion and the Unicorn,* Vol. 24, No. 1, January, pp. 97–109.

Tefferteller, R. (1959) 'Delinquency Prevention Through Revitalizing Parent-Child Relations,' *The Annals of the American Academy of Political and Social Science,* Vol. 322, March, pp. 69–78.

Thacker, D. and Webb, J. (2002) *Introducing Children's Literature: From Romanticism to Postmodernism,* New York: Routledge.

'The Now and Future Queen' (1966) *Time,* 23 December, pp. 53–7.

'The World Premiere of Mary Poppins (1964)' (2016) *DisneyAvenue.com,* 1 September, https://www.youtube.com/watch?v=U0neYmL24ps.

Tims, A. (2013) 'How We Made Mary Poppins,' *Guardian,* online, 2 December, www.theguardian.com/film/2013/dec/02/how-we-made-mary-poppins.

Tinee, M. (1964) 'Julie Leading a Hectic Life, But on Her it Looks Good,' *Chicago Tribune,* 1 November, p. G11.

Tonkin Gulf Resolution (1964) H.J. Res. 1145, 88th Cong, https://www .ourdocuments.gov/doc.php?flash=true&doc=98&page=transcript.

Travers, P.L. (1926) 'Mary Poppins and the Match-Man,' *The Christchurch Sun,* 13 November.

Travers, P.L. (1965) 'A Radical Innocence,' *New York Times,* 9 May, pp. 1, 38.

Travers, P.L. (1975) 'On Not Writing for Children,' *Children's Literature,* Vol. 4, pp. 15–22.

Travers, P.L. (1980) 'Only Connect,' in V. Havilland (ed.), *The Openhearted Audience: Ten Authors Talk About Writing for Children,* Washington, DC: Library of Congress, pp. 3–23.

Travers, P.L. (1988a) 'Something Else,' *Parabola,* Vol. 13, No. 3, Fall, pp. 30–2.

Travers, P.L. (1988b) 'Personal View; Books,' *Sunday Times,* 11 December, p. G4.

Travers, P.L. (1997) *Mary Poppins,* Boston, MA and New York: Sandpiper (Houghton Mifflin Harcourt). Originally published in 1934.

Travers, P.L. (2014a) *Mary Poppins Comes Back,* in P.L. Travers (ed.), *Mary Poppins Collection,* New York: Houghton Mifflin Harcourt, pp 209–498 (originally published in 1935).

Travers, P.L. (2014b) *Mary Poppins Opens the Door*, in P.L. Travers (ed.), *Mary Poppins Collection*, New York: Houghton Mifflin Harcourt, pp. 501–753 (originally published in 1943).

'Walt Disney Accused' (1965) *Horn Book*, Vol. 41, 7 December, pp. 602–11.

'Walt Disney's Radio Interview for the New York World's Fair (1964)' (2008) *YouTube*, online, https://youtu.be/PuonSVNCpZE.

Watts, S. (2001) *The Magic Kingdom: Walt Disney and the American Way of Life*, Columbia, MO: University of Missouri Press.

Weygandt, C. (1904) 'The Irish Literary Revival,' *The Sewanee Review*, Vol. 12, No. 4, October, pp. 420–31.

White, D.N. (1949) *About Books for Children*, New York: Oxford University Press.

Whyte, W. (2002) *The Organization Man*, Philadelphia, PA: University of Pennsylvania Press (originally published in 1956).

Wilson, E. (1964) 'Too Much Sex,' *Austin Statesman*, 29 December, p. 2.

Winslet, K. (2011) 'Todd Haynes,' *Interview* magazine, online 22 February, https://www.interviewmagazine.com/film/todd-haynes.

Zylstra, F. (1965) 'Julie's Best Role: Homemaker,' *Chicago Tribune*, 12 March, p. B12.

Index

3 20